TEACH YOUR SELF POOL based ⟨...teachings of⟩
C.Raftis.

For further information write to: C.R.Billiards, P.O.Box
02903, Detroit, Michigan, 48202, USA.

Wc. side arm stroke-C.Raftis-Side View

TEACH YOUR SELF POOL (prev. edition CUE TIPS)

Original drawings, text and design by C.Raftis
Technical assistance by Nick Raftis, Saginaw, MI.
Cover design by David Mills, Detroit, MI.
Illustrations by Mathew Breneau, Detroit, MI.
Verifications by K. A. Rogers, St Clair Shores
"A" Photographs by David Rennalls, Detroit, Mi.
"A" Photographs and Verifications at Pointe Billiards, 18000 E Warren, Detroit, MI. 48224
"B" Photographs by Stephen Knapp, Detroit, MI.
"B" Photographs taken at Cushion, Cue & Brew, 21901 Kelly Rd, E.Detroit, MI., 48021

Printed in the USA

Published in Detroit, Michigan, USA by C.R.Billiards, P.O.Box 02903, Detroit, Mi, 48202.

ISBN 1-880135-00-0

Greg Dudzinski follow through   -angle view

Dedicated to those individuals who desire to do more than just bang the balls around the table and to all the ladies in my life who are the inspiration to engage in commerce by writing and selling this book.

This book would not have been possible without the assistance of Dr. Ray Genick, W.S.U.; Gary Shields, W.S.U.; and Joe Bassett, Royal Oak,   MI.

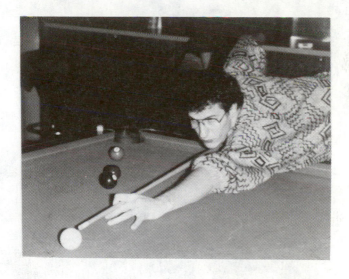

Dominic Zito addressing cue ball   -angle view

Portrait of a Player-Kristie Ann-Front View

TEACH YOUR SELF POOL

Introduction	01
Men, Women, Children, and Handicappers.	03
The Equipment	07
The Basics	11
Glossary of Terms	37
Cue Ball Hits	49
Object Ball Hits	53
The Force Chart	71
How, When and What to Practice	73
Position Play	75
Practice Shots: Beginners & Intermediates	77
Starting the Game	174
Racking and Breaking	178
The Eight Ball Game	182
The Nine Ball Game	186
Practice Shots: Advanced and Expert	194
Fancy Shots	264
Competing	281
Helpful Advice	287
About The Author	299
Mechanical Devices	311
Special Index	317
Diagram index	319
Illustration Index	323
Photographic Index: A	324
Photographic Index: B	326

Lady holding a cue stick-Carol-Close up

INTRODUCTION.

The game of pool has reached such a high degree of popularity, that the pool table has become a requisite in every well furnished modern household, and to play a fine game is regarded as one of the accomplishments of every well educated person. To reach the proficiency of the great experts, is not, of course, easily attainable; however, becomming a good amateur player is not an extravagant ambition. It is within the province of every one gifted with ordinary natural abilities, and aided by a good text-book, which will guide him step by step to master the strokes usually presenting themselves in a game, to reach a degree of skill which will entitle him to rank as an accomplished player. The present book, besides answering such a purpose will be found to be the most perfect work on pool ever offered to todays public. The theory and practice of pool play is clearly explained by numerous diagrams drawn to scale and easily understood. We might add here that without the aid of a good cue, a level table, furnished with accurate cushions, and round, resilient balls, the student will make slow progress. With these, however, assisted by constant practice of the various strokes represented by the diagrams in this work, he or she will soon master the intricacies of the game, and become a good player. To aid every one who has the leisure to devote to this innocent pastime to become such, is the main purpose of this book.

I wish you every success in playing pool. May all the desired object balls roll into the pockets and may you win all your match games. Don't forget that the world of knowledge flows through books; so you have this book, now you must take advantage and learn all that is to be learned from this book.

All the essential information regarding pocket billiards is explained in this book, especially as relates to the subject of pool mathematics. In other words, if it is not in here, then it is not worth noting.

Lady chalking cue-Carol-Front View

MEN,WOMEN,CHILDREN,AND HANDICAPPERS.

Most men have the ability to produce the power stroke or to strike the cue ball so that it travels twice around the table or to strike the cue ball so that it travels five times up and down the table lengthwise. Also men easily have the ability to manage the cue stick with a pendulum stroke and seem to naturally have the ability to hold the cue stick firmly in front and firmly in back in order to control the swing. The other parts of the pool playing public do not naturally take to playing pool and all have some limitations concerning the ability to control the cue stick and to make the power hits. One author reported that men are able to drive the cue ball at a speed of twenty five miles per hour. The author sites an experiment using a TV video tape to estimate the speed of the ball. The same author reports that women strike the ball with less force and that the cue ball only travels at a speed of twenty miles per hour. I agree with the general assumption that most men will be able to apply more force to the ball than most women and that children also would be able to apply less force than a man or woman; maybe again about eighty per cent.

One of the early instructions that I use when teaching is to have a woman or child develop their power stroke by driving the cue ball three rails around the table into a corner pocket. Once they are able to do this then the majority of the shots that occur in a pool game can easily be made as far as the force applied to the shot is concerned. Handicappers or wheelchair users have difficulty with the pendulum stroke. The same difficulty is experienced by young children; for them I recommend the side arm stroke or the modified side arm stroke. Unless a child is a teenager the height might be a handicap in employing the pendulum stroke which is normal among the men players. If a lady is short she may also want to try the side arm stroke or modified side arm stroke. So for people who are short in height I would recommend the side arm stroke or the modified side arm

Child holding a cue stick-Chrissy-Front View

stroke. Now I have been addressing a side arm stroke and a pendulum stroke, most readers I am sure have not heard of this terminology so I will explain. Many of you have watched a baseball pitcher when throwing a fast ball; he throws it side arm. Many of you may have watched a pitcher throwing a soft ball; he throws it underhanded or similiar to the pendulum stroke. Another example of a pendulum stroke is that of an old grandfathers clock or the old stand up clock. It has a pendulum that swings back and forth in order to keep the time.

Another way of understanding a side arm stroke is by the position of the forearm. In the sidearm stroke the forearm is parallel to the floor and in the pendulum stroke the forearm is perpendicular to the floor. Some examples of these different strokes may be viewed in some of the photos that are illustrated in this book.

In addition to stroking which is very important, there is also the grip at the front and rear of the cue stick. In the front the rule is to apply as much pressure as you can and still allow the cue to slide through the fingers. In the back the rule is to be firm but loose; in other words, to control the swing of the cue but still allow the use of the wrist on some shots. You don't want to play with a stiff wrist because it will be more tiring and the manipulation of the cue will be less effective. So again the rule is tight in front and slightly loose in the back to allow proper cue control.

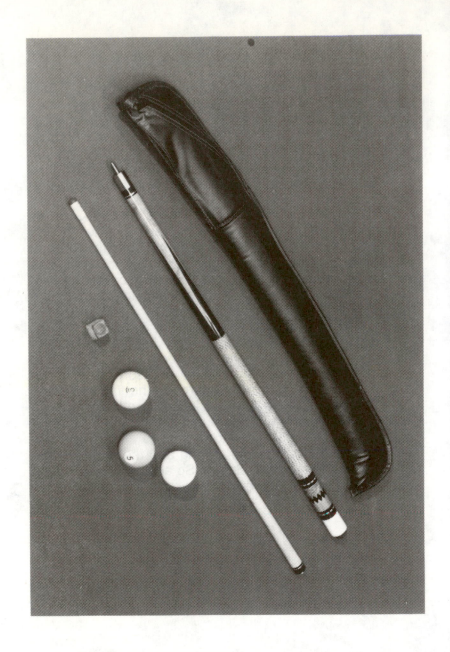

Display Pocket Billiard Equip.-Raftis-O.H.

THE EQUIPMENT, THE TABLE, THE CUES, THE BALLS, THE CHALK, THE BRIDGE, THE CUE TIP, THE CLOTH, AND THE LIGHTS.

Let's discuss the table. A table consists of legs, a bed (normally of slate), rails (normally of wood), rubber cushions attached to the rails, pockets fixed at the ends of the rails and in the middle of the long rails, and a cloth covering (normally of wool or wool with a backing). The sizes vary from three feet by six feet to five feet by ten feet. Of course there are some smaller sizes and there are some larger sizes but they are in such a small minority that they are not considered here. Common sizes are four feet by eight feet and four and one half feet by nine feet. To know how much space you need to place a table in your room just add a five foot perimeter. The size of the table is not exactly what it says. For example a four foot by eight foot table used in a commercial room measures forty four by eighty eight inches on the inside playing surface. Add six inches around the perimeter for the cushion and rails and then the overall size of the four foot by eight foot commercial table would measure fifty six inches wide by one hundred inches long or a little bigger than four feet by eight feet. The important thing to remember about the table is that it needs to be level and that the rubber cushions should give a natural bounce to the ball. Relevelling the table or replacing the rails after installation is a possibility.

Speaking about cue sticks, there are many companies manufacturing cue sticks which are reliable. Some cue manufacturers have been in the business for a long time and have a reputation to back up their display of cues and the cue's performance. Of course an expert player may be able to shoot with a crooked house cue and perform exceptionally well. A new player will have to seek advice from an experienced player or from an experienced dealer in cues in order to find the cue that has just the right feeling in the hand. Some things to keep in mind when cue shopping are that you may roll the cue on a level surface and if it wobbles, then the cue is not straight. The best cues are made with air-dried aged wood and are made by craftsmen. These cues are personalized and are normally expensive when compared with the kiln dried cues that are mass produced. One thing to look for in a cue is a metal joint instead of a plastic one. Another thing to look for is a tip that is glued on instead of slipped on or screwed on. The balance of the cue is important. The balance should be near where you would normally hold the cue. Check the balance by running your index finger along the cue while holding the rear of the cue lightly with your other hand; when both ends of the cue sit on your index finger then the cue is balanced at that point. For many players the balance point will be in front of the hand position that holds the rear of the cue; this then allows the cue tip to be normally lower than the rear of the cue which in most cases is desirable.

The balls are basically plastic cast pheonelic resin. There are two ball sets that are preffered. One is Super Crystalite and the other is Brunswick Centennials, both are produced by Belgian Aramith Ball Company of Belgium.Look for vivid colors. Another thing to look for is the reconstitution properties of the balls. Bang them together and listen for the clicking noise. The "click" means that the ball is reconstituting itself. There is a story of one blind person who was listening to a match between Willie Hoppe and another player and the blind person could tell who had shot the last shot by the sound of the click that the balls made upon contact. Players who used to perform exhibitions used to carry their balls with them. It would take several sets of balls to make one good exhibition set because of the natural balance of the ball. Each ball is not perfect because they are made in large production lots; therefore, each ball is an individual and may not have the same roll or balance as another ball even within the same set. This statement is true about the pool game in general in that even the tables, cues, balls, etc. are not perfect and that they are each an individual and need to be treated as such. Sometimes it is said that to play a player on his home table or his own table gives him an advantage. This would not be true if the tables and balls were always the same.

breaking apart or that is too hard when applied to the cue tip then you need to replace that chalk with a superior brand. Chalk that is normally used in a pool room or pocket billiard lounge is normally of usable quality. If when you brush the pool table you are always brushing up bits and pieces of chalk then you should change the chalk. Sometimes you may notice the chalk being gritty; this could be chalk that needs to be thrown away and replaced. I always keep a few pieces of usable chalk with me and then I always have a consistent chalked surface on the cue tip. You may ask how often should the cue tip be chalked. There is not a correct answer. Different players will give different answers. Some players chalk their cue before every shot. Others chalk their cue every few shots. The important thing to remember is that the chalk provides an abrasive film on the cue tip. When the cue tip contacts the hard polished surface of the cue ball it will make a good, firm contact and not slide off. The tip is not being chalked enough if you are miscueing or sliding the tip off the cue ball upon impact. Do not grind the chalk onto the cue tip. This activity may remove more chalk than it applies. Rather wipe the chalk onto the cue tip evenly so that it is smooth.

The mechanical bridge is sometimes called the "farmers aid" or a "crutch". If a player is not able to make a good finger bridge for the cue then the player can use the mechanical bridge instead. The mechanical bridge for that player then would be a "crutch" or an aid to bridging. The best way to use the mechanical bridge is to place it firmly on the table. Place the front end of the cue on top of the mechanical bridge; hold the bridge with one hand affixing it to the table surface, and then by lightly holding the end of the cue stick you are ready for the stroke. An important point to remember is that you should have the cue tip as close as possible to the cue ball. If the cue tip is some distance from the cue ball the chances of error become greater in striking the cue ball where you desire. Some players are reluctant to use the mechanical bridge. Everyone should learn how to use the bridge properly. Sometimes it is necessary to hold the bridge in an elevated position in order to perform a proper sighting of the shot or because the table is crowded with object balls and there is no place to rest the bridge. The rule is whenever possible hold the bridge firmly in place on the table surface.

Lighting is very important. If you are interested in economy you will want to use florescent tube bulbs. They are best used in a fixture that has a covered bottom so as to eliminate any eye glare. Iridescent bulbs can be used but they must be completely covered as the glare from iridescent bulbs is quite great. If you happen to play in an area that has open or uncovered iridescent bulbs you may want to wear eye glasses with a tint or even sunclasses to reduce the amount of glare. There are many desirable fixtures on the market. Most of them are decorator styled for the recreation room. Many of the pool lounges today offer decorator lighting. Most all lighting offered is bulb; florescent tube fixtures must be special ordered. The lighting fixture should adequately illuminate the table from the head to the foot. The fixture should hang thirty one inches from the table surface to the edge of the shade for the least amount of shadow and glare.

John Beyerlin on follow through   -side view

THE BASICS.

The stance is very important in that by a proper stance you are able to position your body in line with the shot pattern. The stance is performed by standing ninety degrees to the line of the shot, then leaning over towards the shot with the head over the line of the cue stick. Next you need to move the forward foot forty five degrees towards the shot. Now turn the head slightly to favor the coordinating eye; that is the right eye if you are left-handed and the left eye if you are right-handed. Next the bridging and holding of the cue. The forward hand is the bridge hand. If you are a beginner then you may want to make a fist and place the fist onto the table surface. Then crook your thumb against the index finger. The cue will now fit into the groove between your thumb and index finger. To strike the cue ball in different positions it is only necessary to turn the wrist to change the position of the cue. The rear hand is now used to propel the cue forward. Cup the rear of the cue in the palm of the rear hand. Make a circle with the thumb and index finger. This circle will help to hold the cue and leave the wrist to move freely. Hold the body steady and move the cue forward from the elbow. The quicker you accelerate the movement of the cue the stronger the force applied to the cue ball and subsequently to the object ball. Normally you will want to hold the cue behind the balance point with the rear hand. A few warm up movements may be desirable to give the confidence that you will strike the cue ball properly. You may sometimes desire to hold the cue at the balance point or in front of the balance point in order to facilitate a certain shot pattern. Holding the cue in front of the balance point will lighten the stroke and normally apply less force to the cue ball. In certain instances this may be desirable. Also you may want to hold the cue further back in order to extend your reach for a specific shot pattern. Whatever the case may be you will probably always want the front of the cue to be in a down position in order to strike the cue ball properly so the balance is very important and the speed of stroke is also important.

Being able to shoot with both hands is an advantage. Sometimes for a left-handed person it is hard or difficult to reach the shot but by switching hands the shot becomes less difficult.

One stroke that is used by many experienced players is the slip stroke. The method used is to hold the rear hand forward about five or six inches on the cue from the perpendicular arm position on the pendulum stroke and then just prior to striking the ball, slip the shooting hand back to the perpendicular position; this is called the slip stroke. It is a different style of shooting and may be more effective for one player than for another.

The table can play slow, medium, or fast depending on weather conditions, the age of the cloth, and the viscosity of the rubber rails. The best conditions are a slightly used cloth with slightly warm, dry, weather and a rubber cushion that provides an even bounce when played under normal conditions. If the table plays slow then four and five rail shots may be out of the question and not considered when reading the table. If the rails do not provide an equal bounce and equal angles then a majority of the bank shots may be impossible to execute. If the cloth is considerably worn then rail shots or shots played down the rail on the worn cloth might be quite easy to make. The rule here is to know the table that you are playing on in order to be able to execute the desired shot patterns.

One style of play that has not been mentioned is rifling. The player has his or her head over the line of the cue and sights down the cue as if it was a rifle. What is seen then is the cue ball covering the surface of the object ball and by practicing different variations of ball cover the expert can perform any cut shot patterns that come up. Sometimes with the rifling player the player holds the cue prior to delivery to make a final determination on the shot and then moves the cue forward; this is called cocking the cue.

The aim point is determined by using a phantom cue ball either mentally or physically. Mentally by locating a point on the cloth one and one eights of an inch distant from the desired object ball. Physically by placing an object ball against the desired object ball and in line with the pocket opening. The ball removed from its position on the table may be replaced by marking the spot from which it was removed. Now we have two cue balls on the table. One is the actual cue ball and the other is the phantom cue ball; draw a line through the centers of the two cue balls and extend the line to the rail surface. Place a piece of chalk or a marker on the center of the extended line and remove the object ball used as a phantom cue ball. Now align the cue stick through the center of the cue ball and in line with the aim point. Execute the shot by maintaining your body position and pressing the cue forward on the line of aim.

I would like to mention how to take care of the equipment used in playing pool. The cue stick is easily taken care of by occassionally wiping it down with a damp cloth to remove dirt and imbedded chalk. Having a cue case helps to keep the cue from absorbing moisture and dust. I don't agree with sanding or removing the finish from the cue in order to get a better feel. By removing the finish you allow the moisture to enter the cue and subsequently for the cue to warp on the shaft end. The tip may need the use of a hard file or a scraper to keep the tip surface from becomming hard and glossy and to allow the tip to receive the abrasive chalk. The balls also need to be wiped clean with a damp cloth. Many pool rooms have ball polishers.

Stance and Line up-Kristie Ann-Side View

14

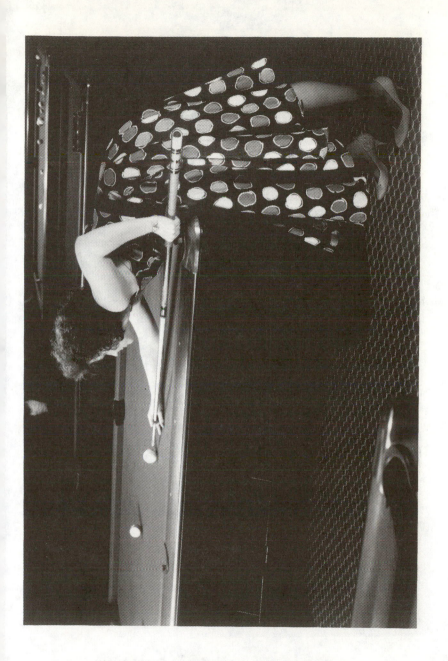

Stance and Line up-Kristie Ann-Side View

Lady playing a corner shot-Carol-Front View

Ladie's Stance and Position-Carol

Stance and Stroking position -Carol-Rr. View

18

Child stroking cue ball-Clint-Side View

Normal Stroke-Pendulum Pos.-Raftis-Rr View

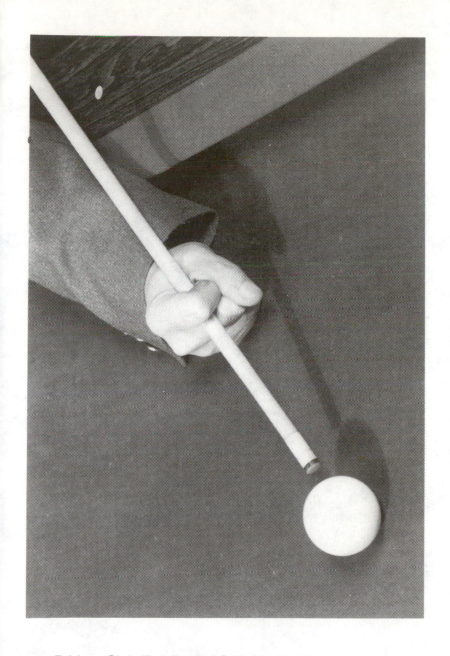

Bridge -Club Fist Follow-C.Raftis-Frt View

Bridge -Club Fist center ball-Raftis-Frt View

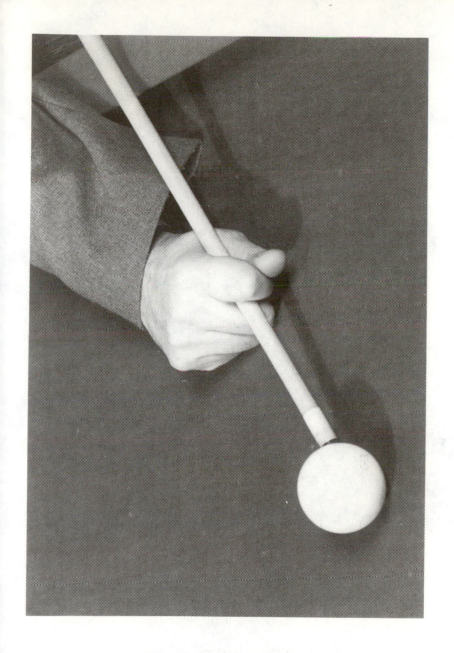

Bridge -Club Fist Draw-C.Raftis-Frt View

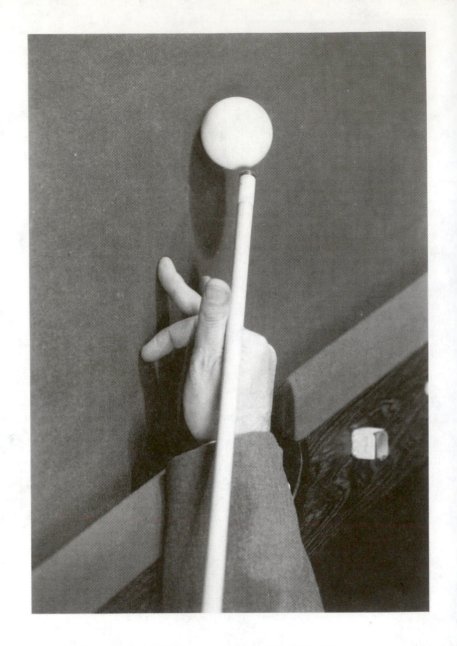

Bridge Hand-"V" Groove-C.Raftis-Side View

24

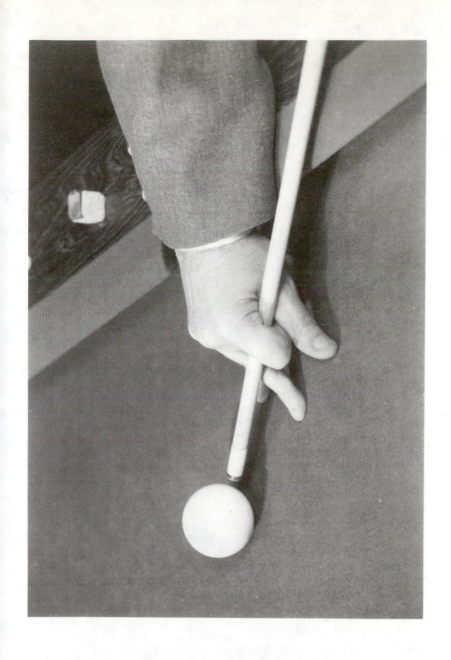

Bridge -Short "Hoppe"-C.Raftis-Side View

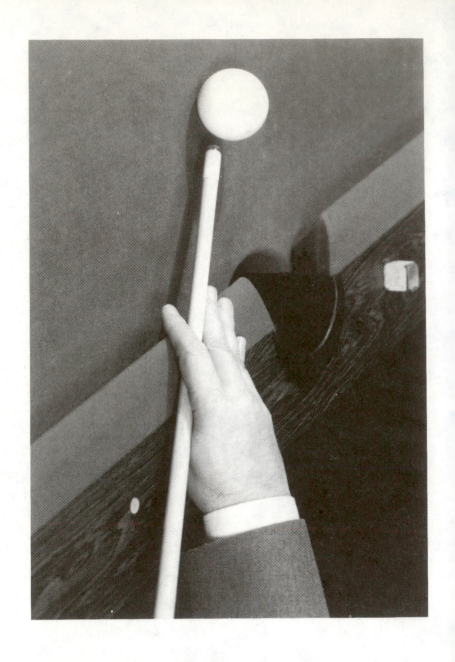

Bridge Hand-Overlap finger -Raftis-Side View

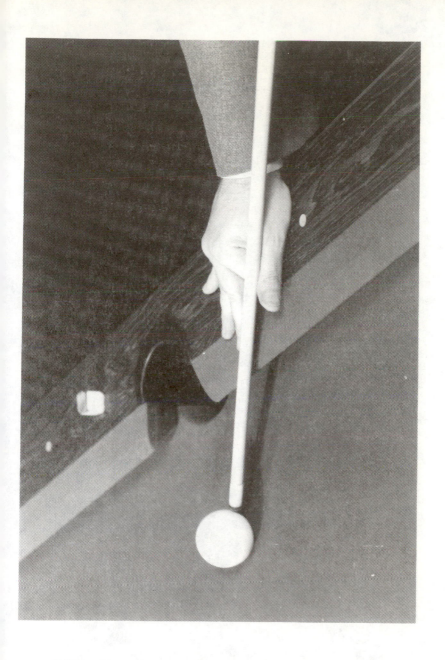

Bridge Hand-Over thumb-Raftis-Side View

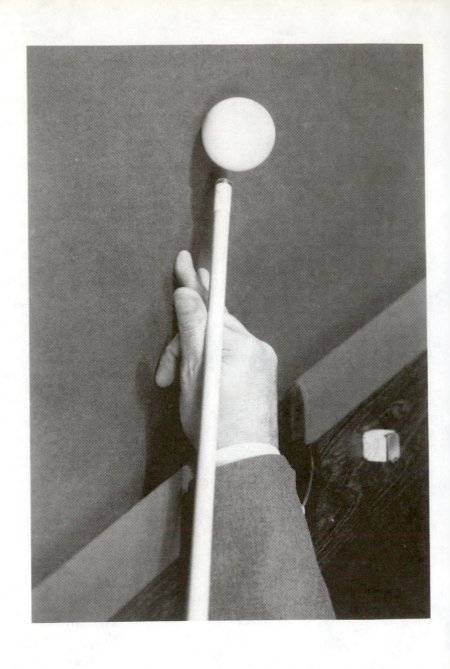

Bridge -Over the thumb-C.Raftis-Side View

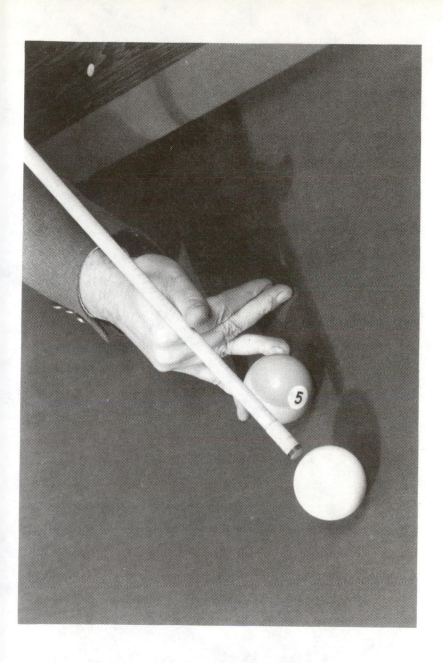

Bridge - shooting over ball-Raftis- Frt View

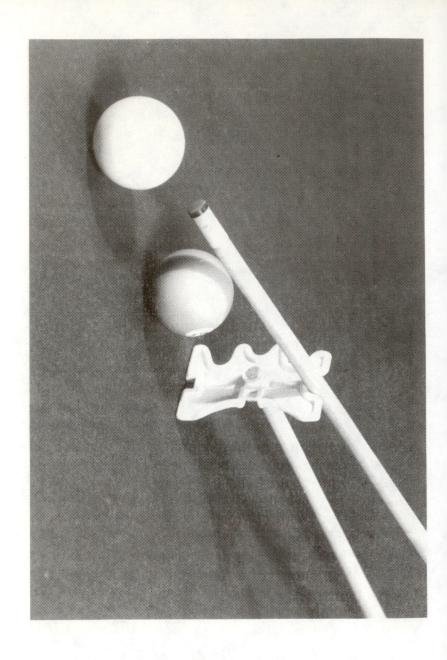

Mech Bridge over a ball-C.Raftis-Close up

Mech Bridge-Long Reach-C.Raftis-Frt View

Child using a milk box -Chrissy-Frt View

Mech.Bridge-over a ball-Raftis- Frt View

Portrait of a lady pool player-Carol-Frt View

Lady using mechanical bridge-Carol-Frt View

Hand Pos. for the Slip Stroke-Raftis-Rr View

36

A GLOSSARY OF TERMS.

ANGLE - A deviation from a straight line.

ANGLE OF INCIDENCE - The angle formed when a ball strikes the rubber cushion from the balls' starting point.

ANGLE OF REFLECTION - The opposite angle to the angle of incidence when the ball strikes the rubber cushion without spin or influence. The angle of reflection is equal to the angle of incidence when the ball striking the cushion turns over after being struck in the dead center or at the junction of the horizontal and vertical dividing lines.

APEX BALL - The apex ball is the front ball in the rack and it is situated on the foot spot or the spot affixed to the table at the far end.

BALANCE - The place on the cue where you place your finger and both ends of the cue are in balance or the weight is evenly distributed.

BALL BANGERS - The majority of pool players who are not serious about playing pool but only play to be socially active or to act out their aggressions by knocking balls around the table, sometimes hoping that if they hit the ball hard enough that it will eventually flop into a pocket.

BALL ON - Means that by looking at a group of balls you may find that one ball in the group is on the pocket meaning that by striking the group in a certain manner the "ball on" will be thrown into a pocket.

BANK SHOT - Driving an object ball to one or more cushions.

BILLIARDS - Striking a sphere with a tapered instrument and playing on a table without pockets. Pocket billiards then is a game where the balls are struck with a cue and pocketed on a billiards' table that has pockets attached.

BILLIARD HALL - A room where billiard tables are maintained for play by the public.

BILLIARD LOUNGE - A billiard hall that has been decorated with decorator lights, carpeting and a snack bar. Billiard lounges cater to women, children and families; whereas, a billiard hall is normally frequented by men.

BLACK BALL - The black ball is also known as the eight ball.

BODY FORCE - The use of body force is confined to the break shot and even though commonly used, body force may not be necessary to effectively execute the break shot.

BREAK - To strike a cluster of balls with the cue ball or to break out a cluster of balls with an object ball in order to facilitate a run out.

BREAK SHOT - To strike the rack of balls with the cue ball.

BRIDGE - A mechanical device with grooves to hold the front of the cue or the position of the non-stroking hand in balancing or holding the front of the cue stick.

CALLED BALL - A designated ball in call shot or call pocket.

CALLED POCKET - Designating a pocket for a called ball or desired ball.

CANNON - (British)- When the cue ball strikes two or more balls it is called a cannon.

COCKED CUE STICK - Means that the cue is held temporarily on the back swing of the stroke for a final determination of the shot pattern.

CONSECUTIVE ORDER - Following a numberical sequence or a pre-planned sequence numbered mentally by the player.

CORNER SEWED - Means that the corner of the pocket obstructs the path of the cue ball to the object ball; in other words, the cue ball has entered far enough into the pocket for the edge of the rail at the pocket opening to provide a hazard in making the shot pattern.

CUE BALL IN HAND - Your opponent has fouled; therefore, you are allowed to pick up the cue ball and place it anywhere on the table to your best advantage. This rule is normally found in nine ball and is effective on every shot after the break shot.

CUEING - Moving the cue stick forwards and backwards prior to striking the cue ball; also known as stroking.

CUSHION - The rubber that is attached to the rail. In pocket billiards or pool there are six rubber cushions.

DEAD BALL - When the cue ball is struck in the center or at the junction of the horizontral and vertical dividing lines with a level cue and the cue ball is struck with sufficient force then the cue ball will "stop dead" upon contact with the object ball.

DEGREE OF ADJUSTMENT - When the desired object ball and the cue ball are in a line with a desired pocket then the degree of deviation between the object ball and the pocket is equal to the degree of adjustment for aligning the cue stick with the cue ball.

DEGREE OF DEVIATION - The angle formed when a line is drawn between the object ball and the center of a favorable pocket with a connecting line drawn from the center of the object ball to the area of deviation from the center of the pocket. This statement is only true when the desired object ball obstructs the path of the cue ball with a desired pocket.

DIAMOND - A mark on the table that identifies an equal division of the table. Originally all the marks were diamond-shaped; today there are various marks locating the natural divisions of the tables.

DISCOUNT - A form of handicapping. If I am the better player then I may agree to discounting, which means that my opponent's score is added to his count and at the same time subtracted from my count.

DOUBLE - (British)- A double means a one rail bank shot.

DOUBLE KISS - When a ball strikes the same ball twice during one shot pattern then it is called a double kiss.

DRAW - To put backspin on the cue ball by striking the cue ball below the horizontal dividing line with a quick snappy stroke.

DRIFT - Drift means to float or in other words when a ball is moving slowly on the table it may divert from a true course due to an influence on the ball. The influence may be due to faulty manufacture or to an influence by another striking ball or the cue ball. The cue ball also may drift or float due to the same reasons.

DUCKING - Means to not shoot out at the shot pattern and to play safe or a half safety.

ENGLISH - When a ball deviates from a straight path after being struck then that ball is said to be under the influence of english. Also by striking the cue ball off the perpendicular dividing line, english, influence or spin is applied.

FANNING - To hit an object ball so thin as to blow it into a pocket is called fanning.

FAVORED POSITION - The position on the table where you place the cue ball after your opponent has fouled in the game of nine ball.

FISH - An innocent player who is consumed by a pool sharp or "shark".

FLOAT - Means to drift or move in other than a straight line. This can be caused by table conditions; manufacturing defects; or by an influence placed on one ball by another ball

FLUKE - (British)- A lucky shot. Something out of the ordinary

FOLLOW - Means to strike the cue ball above the horizontal dividing line.

FOOT OF THE TABLE - The far end of the table from where the game started or the opposite end from where the manufactuer's name plate is attached.

FOOT RAIL - The rail at the far end of the table from where the game is started and where the counters are located and under which you might find the rack for racking the balls.

FOOT SPOT - The adhesive cloth or paper disc attached to the cloth at the foot of the table.

FOOT STRING - An imaginary or drawn line from the center of the foot spot to the center of the foot rail. For all practical purposes you will not find a foot string marked on a table. A foot string is used for specific games that are not normally in play at this time.

FOUL - A foul is something that happens out of the ordinary or something that should not have happened. Examples of a foul are: jumping the cue ball or an object ball off the table (without their subsequent return); pocketting the cue ball; moving a ball accidentally with the body or the cue and replacing it without your opponent's consent; striking the wrong ball in the consecutive order; not striking the desired object ball or striking your opponent's ball by mistake; and to not drive a ball to a rail after the initial contact.

FORCE - an application of movement applied to the cue ball or an object ball.

FREEZE OUT - Means that one player has put everything at stake on the outcome of one match set of games.

FRONT RUNNER - A player who is able to win a few fast games and then remain unchallenged is a front runner.

FROZEN - Means that a ball is in contact with another ball or a cushion.

FULL STRENGTH SHOT - Normally associated with the break shot and it means to propel the cue stick into the cue ball in such a manner that you use all your strength to accomplish the shot pattern.

HANDICAPPING - To give your opponent a head start, lead or spot or to minimize your playing abilities is called handicapping and is necessary if you are the better player.

HARD - A designated force of the ball or a difficult shot.

HAZARD - (British)-Pocketing a ball.

HEAD OF THE TABLE - Where the game starts.

HEAD RAIL - Normally where the manufacturer's identity plate is imbedded.

HIGH RUN - A total of the points or balls pocketed in succession.

HOLING - (British)- Pocketing a ball.

HUG - A ball is said to be hugging the cushion when it moves along the cushion lightly touching it.

HUSTLING - To take advantage of your opponent by not revealing your true strength as a player.

JACKED UP - To play with the cue stick held in the air; a form of handicapping.

JAW - The inside of the pocket opening.

JUMP - When a ball leaves the table bed it is said to have jumped.

KICK SHOT - To strike a cushion prior to striking a desired object ball is called a kick shot.

KISS - When two balls strike each other twice usually resulting in a missed shot.

LAG - Rolling a ball to the end of the table and back to the starting position is called a lag. A lag is also a soft hit on the cue ball; such as, force one or two.

LINE BALL - When an object ball's center is on the head string line.

LIVE BALL - A ball that is on the table and in play.

LOCK UP - A player is said to be "locked up" when he has virtually no chance to win; in other words, the player is outclassed.

MAKING A PLAN - To make a plan on how to run out a sequence of balls after reading the table.

MECHANICAL BRIDGE -A device for bridging the cue.

MILKING THE GAME - Winning a percentage of games in order not to be recognized as the better player.

MISQUE - When the cue tip slips off the cue ball at impact.

MISS - When the cue ball fails in it's objective.

MULTIPLE BANK ANGLES - To strike two or more cushions with a ball.

NATURAL - A name given to an easy shot.

NO COUNT - A form of handicapping. For example: I will make ten balls in a row or my score will not count.

NO HIT - Means failure to strike the desired ball.

NOMINATED BALL -Same as a called ball or designated ball.

NUMBERED BALLS - Plastic or ceramic balls with a number imprinted on the face. In pocket billiards or pool the balls are numbered one through fifteen.

OBJECT BALL ANGLE - The object ball angle is determined by the location of a desired pocket.

OBSTRUCTING BALL - A ball that is in a line between a desired object ball and a favored pocket or between the cue ball and a desired object ball. Also a ball obstructing the path for a desired hit point on a cushion.

OFFENDING PLAYER - A player who has committed a foul.

ON A BREAK - Means making a run.

ON HIS GAME - Means the player is in stroke.

ON A ROLL - Means having a good game; a good series; or winning.

OPEN BREAK - In nine ball it means to try to pocket a ball. In eight ball it means to drive four or more object balls to a rail.

OUT OF STROKE - A player who has lost the technique of striking the cue ball with the cue stick is said to be out of stroke.

PARALLELING - To draw a mental line between the object ball and the cue ball and then aligning the cue stick parallel to that line in order to complete the shot pattern. Also to draw a mental line between a ball and a cushion in relation to a ball track.

PERCENTAGE - Used to determine your ability at cut, kick and bank shots. Knowing your percentage is helpful when reading the table to determine the ultimate shot sequence.

PLAYING OUT - Pocketing the last balls on the table which is also known as "running out".

POCKETING - To cause a ball to enter a pocket.

POINT - That part of the cue to which the cue tip is affixed.

POOL SHARP - (British)- The same as a hustler.

POSITION - Means to place the cue ball in a favorable place for the next shot. Also to have obtained a favorable place for the next shot. BAD POSITION then is to have the cue ball out of line with the next shot pattern.

PRINCIPAL BALL - The last ball prior to pocketing the game ball. This is the ball that is used for playing position for the final shot. In eight ball it would be the seventh pocketed ball by one player.

PUSH - Allowing the point of the cue to rest on the cue ball after it's initial contact with the object ball.

RACK - Rack refers to two things. First a rack is an instrument used for racking the balls. Second rack is a verb for grouping the balls for the start of the game.

RAIL - That part of the table to which the rubber cushion is attached and to which the table markings are fixed.

READING THE TABLE - To examine the position of the balls and then make a mental shot sequence plan.

RIFLE SIGHTING - Sighting down the cue stick similar to sighting down a rifle barrel.

ROTATION ORDER - Playing the balls in consecutive number sequence; the lowest number first.

RUN - Pocketing a series of balls in succession.

RUN OUT - To pocket all the remaining balls in one shot sequence.

SAFETY - A difficult leave of the balls.

SCRATCH - Means that the cue ball has entered a pocket or it could be a mark indicating a foul stroke.

SCREW - (British)- The same as a draw shot.

SELECTED POCKET - A desired pocket or a designated pocket.

SET UP - When the balls are left by a player to insure an easy shot by the opponent.

SHOOTING OUT - Playing to make every shot on the table.

SHOT PATTERN - A player's preference for a certain shot or a predesignated shot.

SHOT SEQUENCE - A selected grouping of shots preferred by a player

SLIP STROKE - A form of cue manipulation. Some player's prefer to hold the back of the cue slightly forward from their normal striking position and then just prior to the stroke to slip the hand back into the normal position for execution.

SNOOKER - To hide the cue ball from a direct path to the desired object ball.

SPIDER -(British)- A form of a mechnical bridge for shooting over a ball.

SPLIT HIT - Means to hit two balls at the same time and with the same degree of force. This is not a legal hit in nine ball.

SPOT - First, spot means to advance an opponent's score and second, a spot is a round adhesive disc glued onto the table and used for spotting a ball after a foul stroke.

46

SPOTTING - To place one ball on the spot. Spotting additional balls are in the order of the lowest ball first and are placed directly behind the first spotted ball.

SPOT BALL - (British)- The ball resting on the foot spot.

STAB -(British)- Going for a difficult shot.

STRING LINE - An imaginary or drawn line at the head of the table which offers a restricted space in which to play the balls.

STROKING - The warm up exercise prior to striking the cue ball.

STROKING ARM - For a right handed player it is the right arm and for a left handed player it is the left arm.

STUN - (British)- A dead ball hit struck hard.

THROW - To influence a ball to travel in other than a straight line.

WING SHOTS - A practice shot to improve hand-eye coordination. Also a series of shots played for an exhibition. The idea is to hold two balls in hand; roll one down the center of the table and before the ball arrives at the end rail, to strike it by shooting the other ball in hand; in other words it is a time shot or a series of time shots.

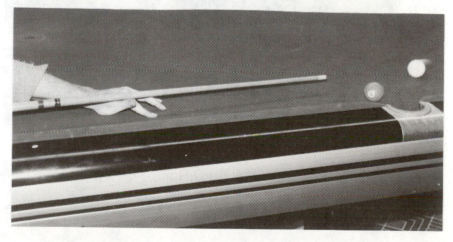

John Beyerlin on follow through   -side view

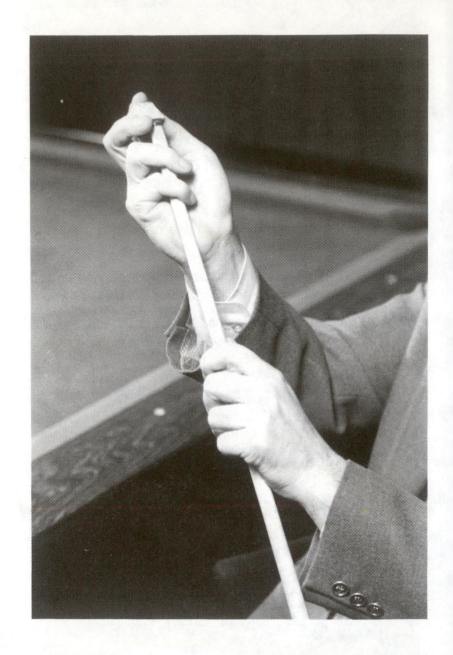

Proper Chalking of the Tip-C.Raftis-Frt View

48

THE CUE BALL HITS.

There are ten basic cue ball hits. First and foremost is the center ball hit or striking the cue ball at the junction of the vertical and horizontal dividing lines. This requires practice and some players are more expert at striking the ball in the center. One way to realize if you are striking the ball in the vertical center is to place the cue ball on the head spot or at the center of the head string. Align the cue stick through the center of the cue ball and in line with the center of the end rail. Now strike the ball with sufficient force to travel up and down the table. If the ball returns to the original position then you have struck the ball in the vertical center. If the ball deviates to the right or left of the original position upon return then you have struck the ball to the right or left of the vertical. Once you master striking the ball on the vertical dividing line then you will need to practice a different stroke in order to find the junction between the horizontal and vertical dividing lines or in other words "dead center". Now place an object ball in the center position on the table. The center of the ball should be on the center of the dividing line of the table or a line drawn from the center of the head rail to the center of the end rail or foot rail. Now place the cue ball on the head spot. Align the cue stick through the center of the cue ball and the center of the end rail. Strike the cue ball with a firm stroke. If you are successful then the cue ball will stop and stay at the point of impact with the object ball. If the cue ball continues forward then you have struck the cue ball above the horizontal dividing line. If the cue ball moves backward then you have struck the cue ball below the horizontal dividing line. It is always recommended to practice making dead ball hits as they are very useful in playing pool, especially when making bank-kick shots which we will discuss later.

The next cue ball hit to be learned is the below center hit. By striking the cue ball below center by one cue tip you will be able to stop the cue ball, return the cue ball, or follow with the cue ball depending on the amount of force applied to the shot pattern. In order to not have the cue

49

ball follow the object ball straight into the pocket it is necessary for you to strike the cue ball below the horizontal center by one cue tip and employ enough force for the cue ball to stop in position upon contact with the object ball. This action requires a prior determination when reading the shot as the distances involved in the calculations determine the amount of force required. If the cue ball is a great distance from the object ball then a greater force is required; also, if the object ball is close to falling into a pocket then more force is required on the cue ball. Force will always be determined by the distances involved.

The draw shot is made by striking the cue ball one cue tip below center and using a strong, long follow through or by striking the cue ball one and one half cue tips below center and using less force and follow through. Again a judgement is required based upon distances the cue ball has to travel either to the object ball or away from the object ball. The "nip draw" is for all practical purposes a certainty. Make a fist and with the palm down place the fist on the table. Now make an opening for the cue with the thumb and index fingers. Place the cue through the opening and execute the shot. When making draw shots one objective is to play the cue through the cue ball to a point on the cloth. Sometimes, if the balls are close together, it will not be possible to reach the cloth with the cue tip but under normal conditions it is possible and practical.

Occasionally you may want to follow with the cue ball. Follow means that after striking the object ball the cue ball follows in it's path or follows in the original line the cue ball was travelling prior to impact. This is basic information and is applicable in a majority of cases. Strike the cue ball at least one cue tip above the horizontal dividing line and on the vertical dividing line. Continue on the follow through to hold the cue tip to the surface of the cue ball and apply an upward motion to the cue tip. This movement of the cue will quarantee a good follow action, especially if the cue ball and object ball are in close proximity to one another. Another follow shot is the "force follow". Strike the cue ball one cue tip above the horizontal dividing line and apply an exceptional force to the cue ball. The cue ball will momentarily stop upon contact with the object ball and then follow the original path of the cue ball or if the object ball is struck full then the cue ball will follow the path of the object ball.

If you are a beginner or intermediate player then you may not want to consider striking the cue ball to the right or left of the vertical center line. The reason that you don't want to consider striking the cue ball to the right or left of the center line is that the cue ball will generally deviate from a straight line in it's travels to the object ball and then again deviate after contact with the object ball. Advanced and expert players are able to control this activity with a greater degree of accuracy after a great deal of experience playing with the cue ball. There are some shots were it is practical and low risk to play with a "spinner" and those shots are illustrated in this book. The rule is: if you can avoid striking the ball off center then avoid it to improve the accuracy of your cue ball hit.

I would like to mention the "soft draw". The soft draw is for experienced players and is usually used to play position for the next shot. The soft draw is explained as meaning what it says. Strike the cue ball one and one half cue tips below the horizontal center and use sufficient force for the cue ball to rotate backwards until contact with the object ball. After contact with the object ball the soft draw shot will restrict the movement of the cue ball to a short distance of deflection from the object ball. This shot pattern can be useful but it requires experience in order to make the judgement call and also experience in order to manipulate the cue ball for the shot.

Striking the cue ball above the horizontal dividing line and to the right or left of center will cause the cue ball to rotate on a diagonal axis. For the inexperienced player this can cause a swerve and a lack of control of the cue ball. There may be occasions when striking the ball in such a manner is recommended but they are few and far between and best avoided except by an expert player or by an illustration for a practice shot in this book.

< Vertical dividing line

Horizontal dividing line

Cue Ball Striking Points

1. Dead Center - The junction of the vertical and horizontal lines. Slow forward rotation
2. One cue tip right of center to impart spin. Forward and spins to right.
3. One cue tip left of center to impart spin. Forward and spins to left.
4. One cue tip above center to impart a fast forward motion.
5. One cue tip below center to impede roll of the ball. Slide then forward or stop.
6. Two cue tips below center to impart a reverse motion. Rotates backward and forced forward.
7. One cue tip below and right of center to impart a swerve or drag motion - diagonal rotation to right.
8. One cue tip below and left of center to impart a swerve or drag motion - diagonal rotation to left.
9. One cue tip above and to the left of center to impart a drift motion - influence to left.
10. One cue tip above and to the right of center to impart a drift motion - influence to right.
Note: On the jump shot the ball face is turned upward so that the number one is on the same angle as the cue stick.

OBJECT BALL HITS.

The full hit means that when viewing the object ball from the position of the cue ball, the cue ball will fully cover the view of the object ball. In other words the cue ball will strike the object ball straight on.

The half ball hit is determined by aligning the cue stick through the center of the cue ball and at the outside edge of the object ball. By executing the shot in this manner you automatically make a half ball hit.

The thin hit requires an alignment of the edges of the two balls, the cue ball and the object ball. Draw an imaginary line between the outside edge of the cue ball and the inside edge of the object ball. Now parallel that line of aim in order to strike the cue ball along the vertical center line. Use a quick movement of the cue in order to fan the object ball. Very little movement is given to the object ball by the cue ball as there is no resistance to the path of the cue ball; therefore, it is necessary when making a thin hit to strike the cue ball with a greater force than would normally be necessary. By striking the cue ball in this manner the cue ball will travel a greater distance than on a normal shot thereby increasing the chances of scratching the cue ball. This is one major consideration when making a determination to execute the thin hit shot pattern.

I don't know of a system for making the one quarter ball hit. Of course it is half way between the half ball hit and the thin hit. The quarter ball hit can be predetermined for practice shots by using a table graph and a protractor. A quarter ball hit is shown in an illustration in this book.

There are many other object ball hits and they will be shown in illustrations in this book for your best advantage in practicing the object ball hits.

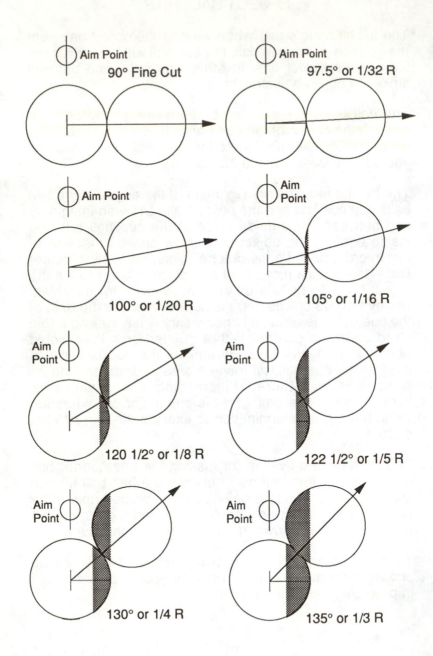

Aim Point
90° Fine Cut

Aim Point
97.5° or 1/32 R

Aim Point
100° or 1/20 R

Aim Point
105° or 1/16 R

Aim Point
120 1/2° or 1/8 R

Aim Point
122 1/2° or 1/5 R

Aim Point
130° or 1/4 R

Aim Point
135° or 1/3 R

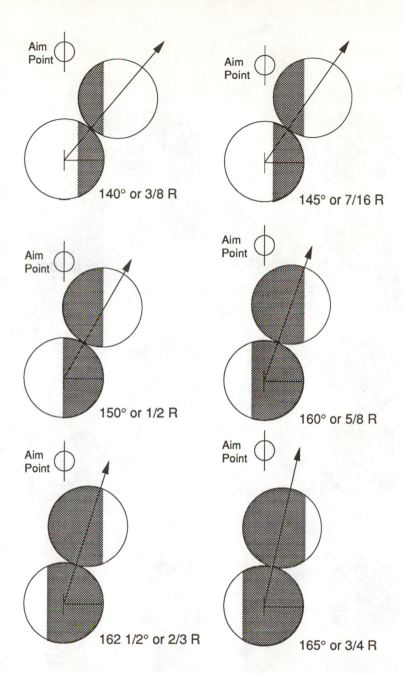

Aim Point   140° or 3/8 R

Aim Point   145° or 7/16 R

Aim Point   150° or 1/2 R

Aim Point   160° or 5/8 R

Aim Point   162 1/2° or 2/3 R

Aim Point   165° or 3/4 R

55

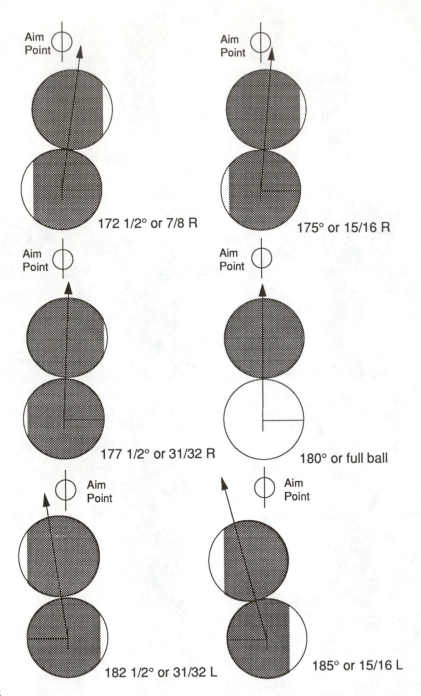

Aim Point — 172 1/2° or 7/8 R

Aim Point — 175° or 15/16 R

Aim Point — 177 1/2° or 31/32 R

Aim Point — 180° or full ball

Aim Point — 182 1/2° or 31/32 L

Aim Point — 185° or 15/16 L

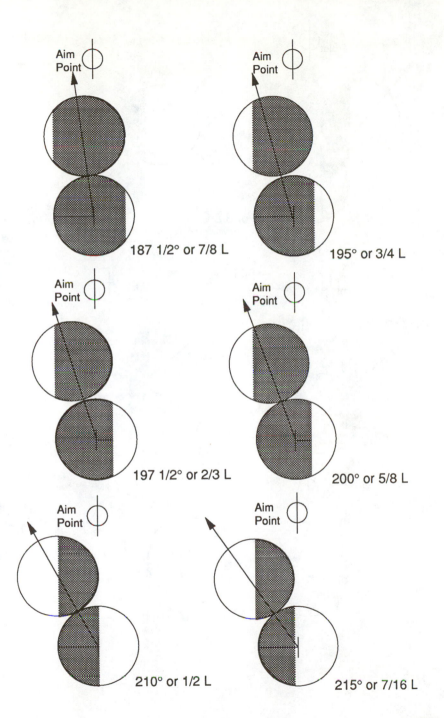

Aim Point — 187 1/2° or 7/8 L

Aim Point — 195° or 3/4 L

Aim Point — 197 1/2° or 2/3 L

Aim Point — 200° or 5/8 L

Aim Point — 210° or 1/2 L

Aim Point — 215° or 7/16 L

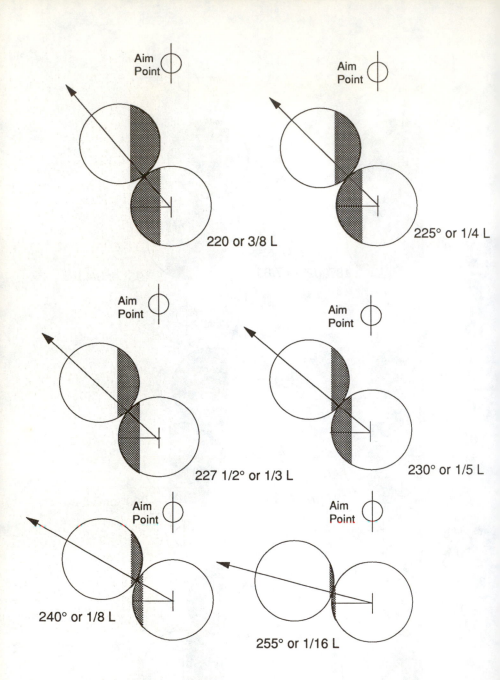

Aim
Point

220 or 3/8 L

Aim
Point

225° or 1/4 L

Aim
Point

227 1/2° or 1/3 L

Aim
Point

230° or 1/5 L

Aim
Point

240° or 1/8 L

Aim
Point

255° or 1/16 L

58

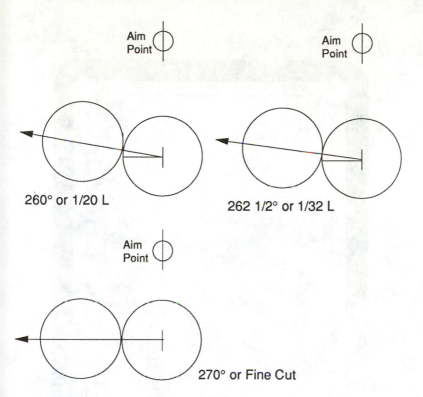

Aim Point

Aim Point

260° or 1/20 L

262 1/2° or 1/32 L

Aim Point

270° or Fine Cut

The circle in line with the aim point represents the phantom cue ball in contact with the object ball. The shadow markings indicate the amount of ball coverage necessary when aligning the shot pattern, in order for the object ball to defect along the path of the arrow. It may be interesting to note that the contact point is different that the aim point and the contact point is in a different relative position with each cut shot pattern. Use these diagrams in conjunction with the billiard protractor and the all purpose chart.

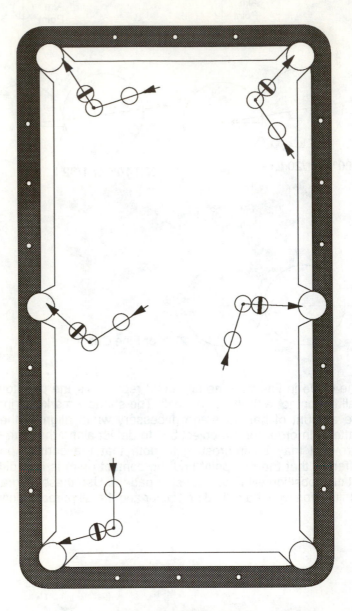

Cut Shot Reference Chart
105° cut or 1/20th
Force no. 1 very soft

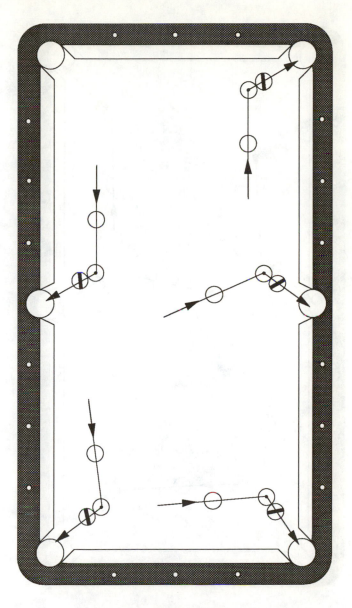

Cut Shot Reference Chart
120° cut or 1/6th
Force no. 1 very soft

61

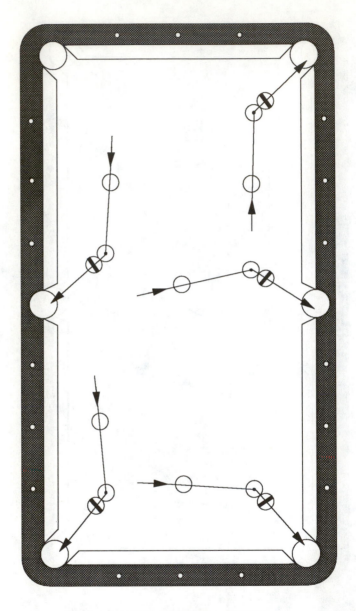

Cut Shot Reference Chart
135° cut or 1/3rd
Force no. 1 very soft

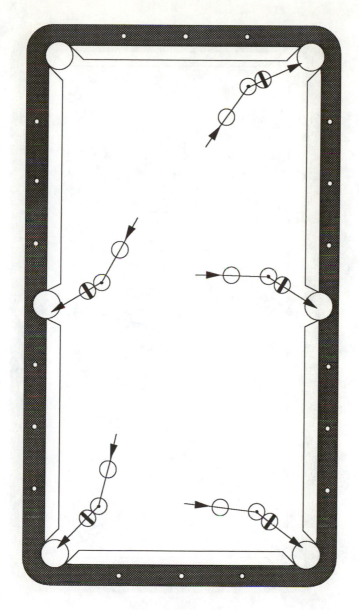

Cut Shot Reference Chart

150° cut or 1/2 ball
Force no. 1 very soft

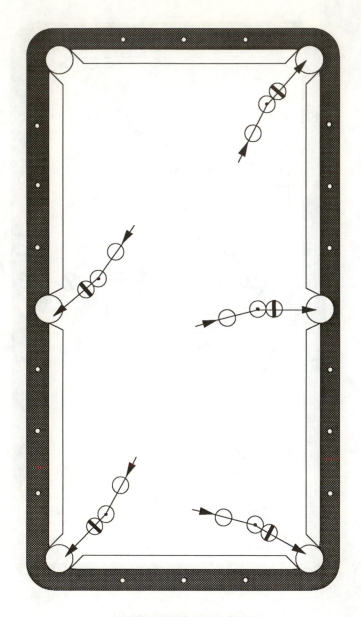

Cut Shot Reference Chart
165° cut or 3/4ths
Force no. 1 very soft

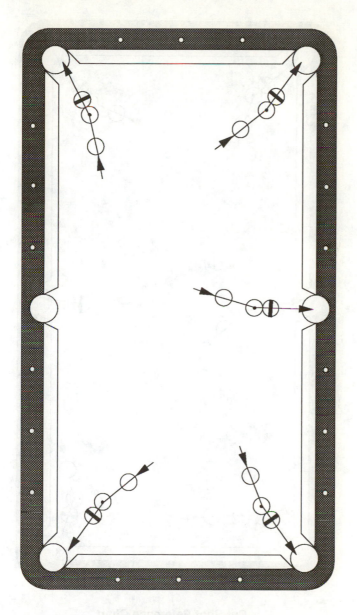

Cut Shot Reference Chart

195° cut or 3/4ths

Force no. 1 very soft

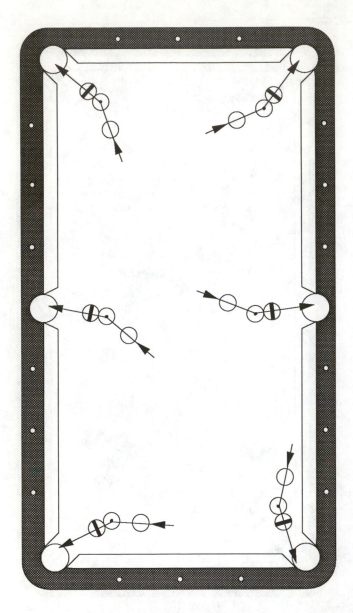

Cut Shot Reference Chart
210° cut or 1/2 ball
Force no. 1 very soft

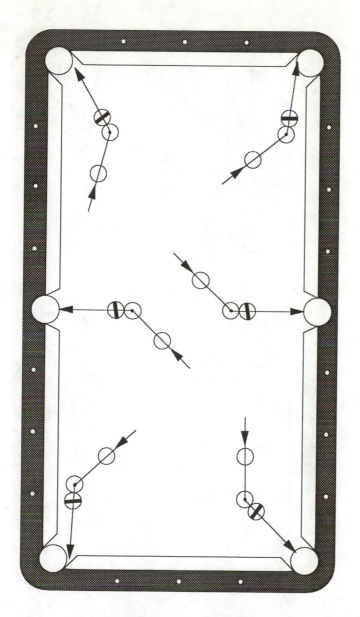

Cut Shot Reference Chart

225° cut or 1/3rd

Force no. 1 very soft

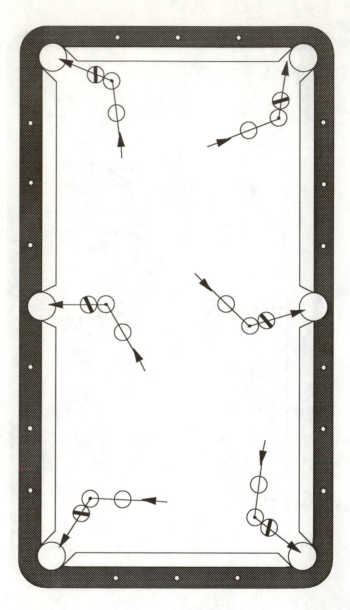

Cut Shot Reference Chart
240° cut or 1/6th
Force no. 1 very soft

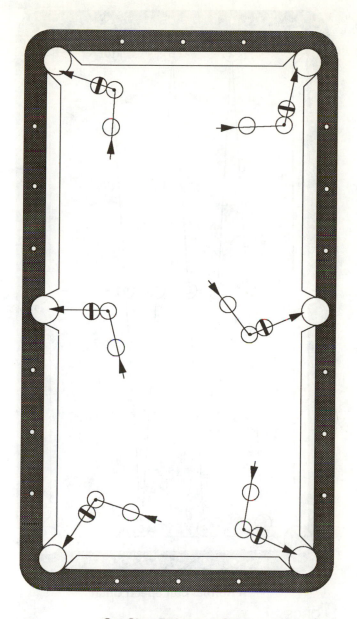

Cut Shot Reference Chart

255° cut or 1/20th

Force no. 1 very soft

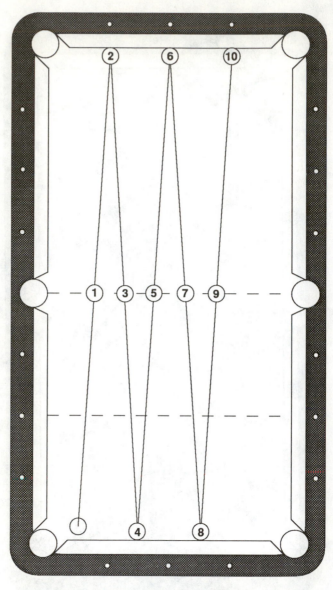

A Normal Ball Speed Chart

FORCE:

No. 1 soft - very easy
No. 2 soft - very easy
No. 3 soft - easy
No. 4 soft - easy
No. 5 medium - moderate

No. 6 medium - moderate
No. 7 hard - strong
No. 8 hard - strong
No. 9 hard - very strong
No. 10 hard - very strong

THE FORCE CHART.

The force chart is decimilated. Force ten is a hard hit ball by an experienced male adult player and the ball should travel on a table with resilient cushions five lengths. Force nine is also a hard hit ball by an experienced male adult player and the ball should travel four and one half table lengths. Force eight is a hard hit ball by an experienced female adult player and the ball should travel four lengths of the table. Force seven is also a hard hit ball by a female adult player that travels three and one half lengths of the table. Force six is a hard hit ball by a child and the ball should travel three lengths of the table. Force five is a similar hard hit by a child and the ball should travel two and one half lengths of the table. Force four is the lag shot which is a soft hit and travels two lengths of the table. Force three is a soft shot and is used quite often for a majority of shots on the pool table. Force three is one and one half lenghts of the pool table. Force two is often used when playing safeties. In force two the ball travels one length of the table. Force one is also a common force and is used when playing a soft lay up. In force one the ball travels one half the distance of the table. Of course other determinations may be made or the ten forces could also be further divided into twenty forces, but from experience if you are able to follow the above force outline you shouldn't have any trouble making your pool shots and playing position for the second shot.

Handicappers, depending on the position of the cue ball, may be restricted in playing shots that require a certain amount of force; therefore, they have to improve their accuracy and maybe make better determinations on how to play a shot when they are not able to make the force requirements.

Child holding a cue stick-Clint-Front View

HOW, WHEN AND WHAT TO PRACTICE.

How to practice is one of the most important topics in playing pool. When you are a beginner or intermediate player it is very important to practice with only the cue ball. Drive the cue ball up and down the table and try to get the cue ball to travel in a straight line. When you are successful at this exercise continue for ten minutes to thirty minutes daily. Another practice shot for beginners and intermediates, actually these practice shots are for everyone but especially for beginners and intermediates, is to bank the cue ball against the cushion to create equal angles. By dividing the area in a square or rectangul you create an equal angle at the point of contact with the cushion. In order for the angle of incidence to equal the angle of relection you must use only sufficient force to allow the cue ball to reach the second rail or a pocket. The force should be enough to go just past the point that you are trying to reach. Another point is that upon contact with the rail the ball will turn over. In other words it is rolling with a forward roll until the rail and then reverses and rolls backwards with a forward roll, because the ball turns over upon contact with the rail. This can be seen by using a striped ball when practicing. You can actually witness the ball rolling one way into the rail and another way after contacting the rail. Another series of practice shots is to place an object ball on an intersecting line dividing the table. There are thirty two squares on the table which are determined by the rail markers. On the table chart lines are drawn from the rail markers and at the intersections of these lines you may place object balls for practice shots. By placing an object ball on one set of intersecting lines and then moving the cue ball to different intersecting lines you will create different shot patterns for practice. If you practice all the shots in this book then you will surely improve your pool game. Try to practice one half hour to two hours daily. If this is not possible try to practice on a regular basis and practice the same warm up exercises. This is the way the champions do it, so you do it and someday you also may become a champion.

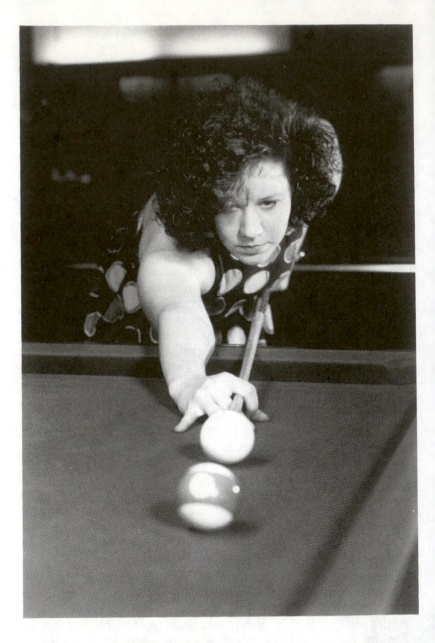

Position of the Head-Kristie Ann-Front View

POSITION PLAY.

One method of playing position is to position the cue ball for a series of draw shots. You draw the cue ball by striking the cue ball below center and through the cue ball to a point on the cloth beyond the cue ball. Use a snappy wrist motion for the best results.

Another method of playing position is to strike the cue ball near the center and move the cue ball the shortest distance towards the desired object ball and in a direction where the object ball would be the shortest distance to the pocket.

A more difficult way of playing position is to try to play the cue ball to come to rest as close to the object ball as practical. This would require the use of various spins on the cue ball and may result in a greater percentage of missed shots.

Another method of position play is to play only the speed of the cue ball for position. In other words the speed of the cue ball is the most important consideration.

Playing the cue ball to put the object ball into the closest pocket is another way of playing position.

One system of playing position is called the "top of the table" system. In this system you try to pocket all of your grouping of balls that are at one end of the table and then go to the other end of the table to complete the run.

The last way to play position is to use all the above techniques according to which will give you the best advantage when running the balls.

Here is one bit of advice when playing position: do not sacrifice pocketing the ball in order to get good position; but always try a little harder to get position when pocketing a ball.

Portrait-pool player standing-Carol-Frt View

PRACTICE SHOTS: BEGINNERS & INTERMEDIATES.

The following shots are illustrated according to the degree of skill needed to perfect the shot. All of the shots illustrated are drawn to scale for a four by eight foot pool table, this being the most common size in use today. The shot patterns are verified, either by an exposed overhead camera shot or by a particpant actually playing and making the shot. So, if you don't succeed the first time, try, try again.

For the bar lounge player, all the shots have been tested on a Valley Recreation table, measuring three and one half feet wide by seven feet long.

So, "have a go". I wish you every success in making all the shot patterns. When you begin making a good percenytage on one shot, then start on the next shot. When you complete the diagrams in this section, then you may start practicing on the more advanced section.

A final note: if you plan to shoot the same shot over and over, then use a removable, self-adhesive ring binder reinforcement to locate the ball.

Richard Clancy prior to stroke   -side view

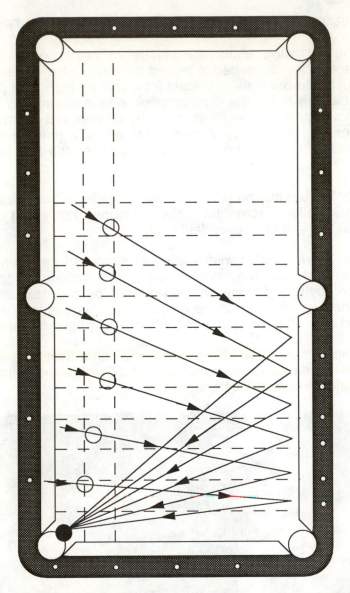

Beginners and Intermediate: angle of incidence = angle of reflection
Kick shot across corner

Place the center of the cue ball on the diagrammed line. Play the shot in the direction of the arrow. Strike the cue ball at the junction of the vertical and horizontal lines; in other words strike the cue ball in the center. Use a soft to moderate stroke using two plus to four plus. Always play the ball to go past the final destination. Hold the cue level during and after striking the cue ball. VERIFIED.

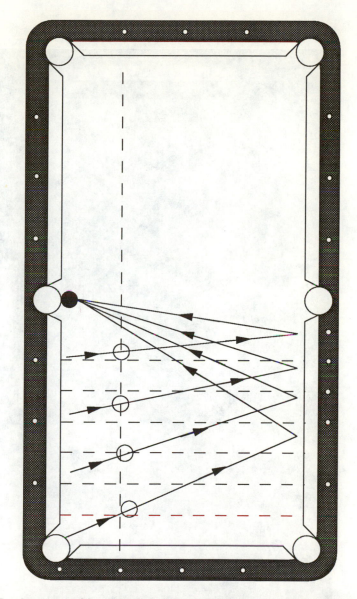

Beginners and Intermediate: The kick shot one rail across side

The diagram shows ball tracks to enter the side pocket. Other ball tracks may be added by paralleling and interpretation. Align the cue stick through the center of the cue ball at the junction of the vertical and horizontal dividing lines and the aim point on the rail. Strike the cue ball with a firm soft stroke using force two and one half to three. Remember that the center line of the cue stick must pass over the center of the rail marker when making the stroke. VERIFIED.

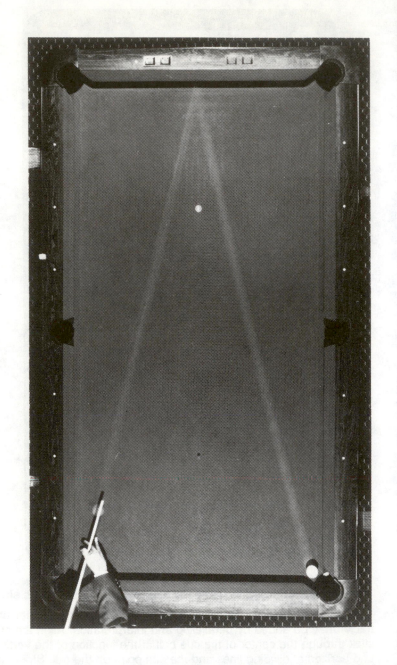

Beg.& Intermediates-Kick -1 rail-Raftis-O.H.

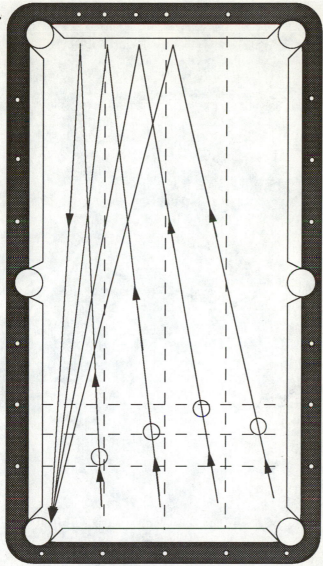

Beginners and Intermediate

angle of incidence = angle of reflection

One rail long into the corner

Strike cue ball at the junction of the vertical and horizontal lines. Center line of cue ball and cue stick must be in relationship to the drawn lines. **Verified see Photo**

81

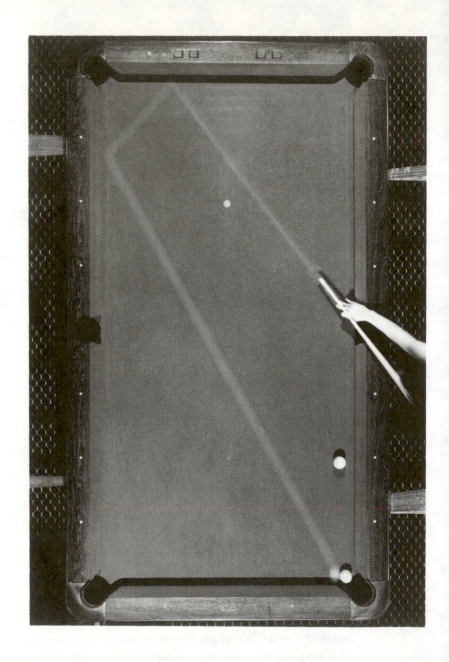

Beg. & Intermediates-Kick Shot 28-K Ann-O.H.

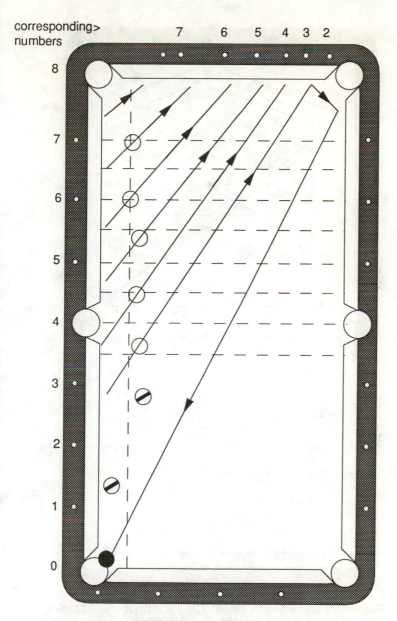

Beginners and Intermediate
The kick shot = two rails in the corner

Place center line of the cue stick over the center of lthe corresponding rail marking. The center of the cue ball must be placed on the digrammed line. On corresponding position number two, strike the cue ball one quarter inch off the vertical center line to the right or one half the diameter of a cue tip to the right. All the other shots are center ball hits. Use forces of three and one half to four and one half or a moderate stroke of the cue. The objective is pocket number two. Verified. Photo

83

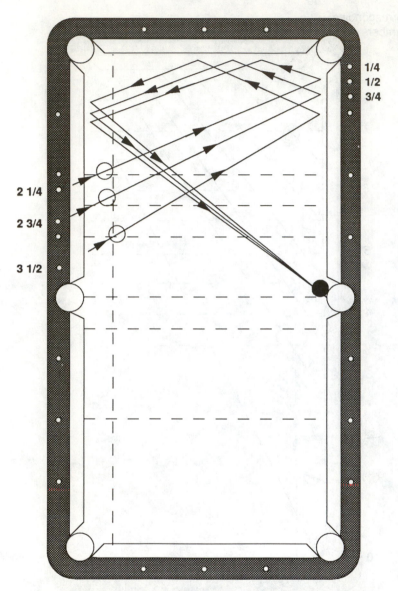

Beginners and Intermediates: The Kick Shot - Ball Tracks
Three rails Short in the Side

This diagram represents the ball tracks for kicking or banking a ball into the side pocket. Strike the cue ball at the junction of the vertical and horizontal divider lines. Employ a firm moderate stroke using force four. Hold the cue level and maintain the body posture until after the ball has contacted the first rubber cushion. Other ball tracks may be made by paralleling or interpreting. Object ball is hit full. VERIFIED.

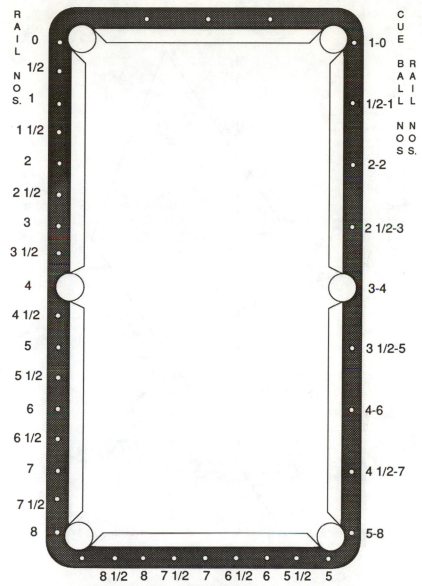

Beginners and Intermediate: diamond system

The essence of the system is that when the back angle is known then by subtracting the back angle rail number from the cue ball position number, then the aim point can be known for a three cushion bank. The aim point for two cushion banks can be known by simply subtracting the desired rail contact from the cue ball position. Always strike the cue ball on a vertical centerline. The position of the cue ball in or near the corner pocket determines the numbering system. Verified.

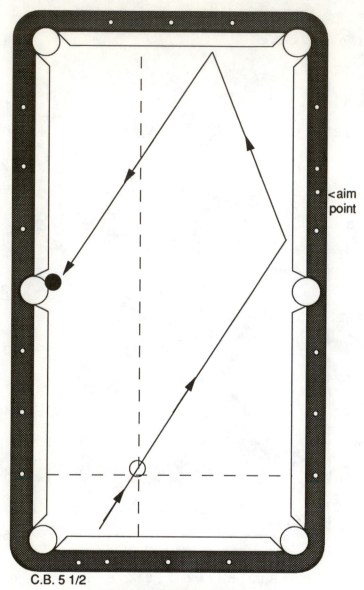

<aim
point

C.B. 5 1/2

Beginners and Intermediate
The kick shot

Place the cue ball on the line from cue ball position five and one half to rail position two and one third. Align the cue stick through the center of the cue ball and in line with the aim point. Strike the cue ball at the junction of the vertical and horizontal dividing lines using force eight. Hold the cue level and employ a hard firm stroke. The cue ball will fly into the side pocket. VERIFIED.

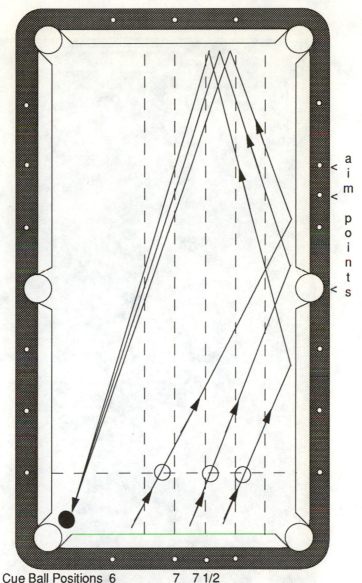

Cue Ball Positions 6   7   7 1/2

Beginners and Intermediate
The kick shot: Two rails long into the corner

The diagram represents the ball tracks for playing kick shots into the corner pocket. Place the cue ball on the center of the reference line. Align the cue stick through the center of the cue ball and in line with the reference point. Parallel that line of aim in order to strike the cue ball to the right of the vertical center by one half a cue tip or one quarter of an inch and on the horizontal dividing line. Employ a moderate stroke using force five. Please note that every table is an individual. Try to practice on the same table for the best results. VERIFIED.

87

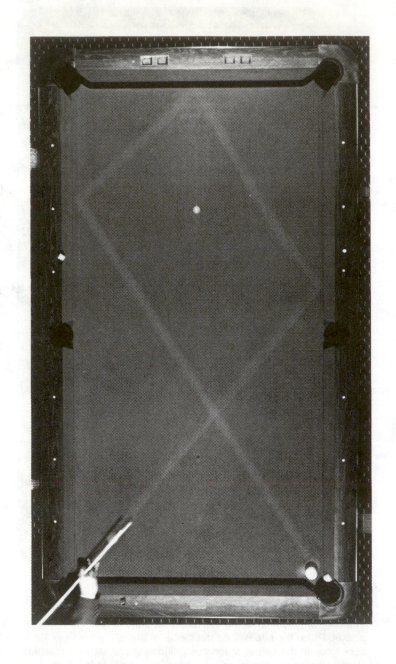

Beg & Advanced-Kick Shot-3 rails-Raftis-O.H.

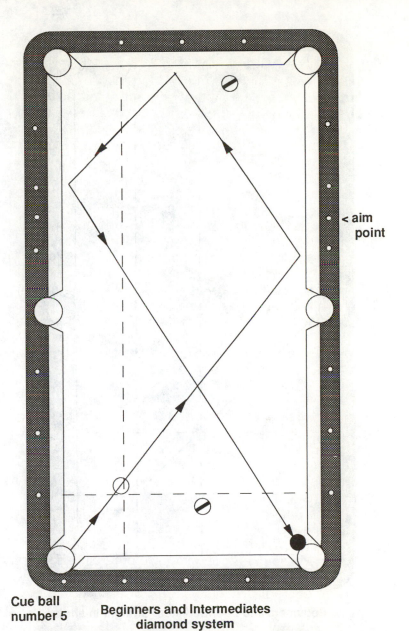

< aim point

Cue ball number 5

Beginners and Intermediates diamond system

The cue ball is located at cue ball position five. Place the center of the cue ball on the drawn line. Strike the cue ball at the junction of the vertical and horizontal lines. Use force five and one half or six, also known as moderate. The objective is pocket number one!The aim point may vary according to the playability of the rubber cushions. VERIFIED PHOTO

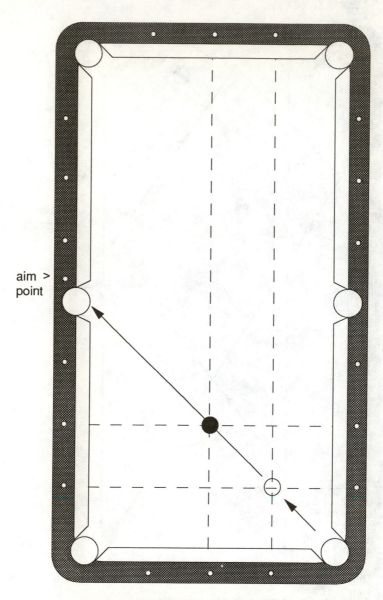

aim >
point

Beginners and Intermediates: Straight in shots

Align the cue stick through the vertical center of the cue ball. Strike the cue ball below the horizontal. Use a soft stroke, or force one and one half. After striking the cue ball, do not raise the cue tip or the body but stay down in position in order to maintain a good follow through. Always play side pocket shots to enter the pocket away from the nearest corner of the pocket. The center line of the cue stick is over the center of the pocket. Object ball is hit full. Verified.

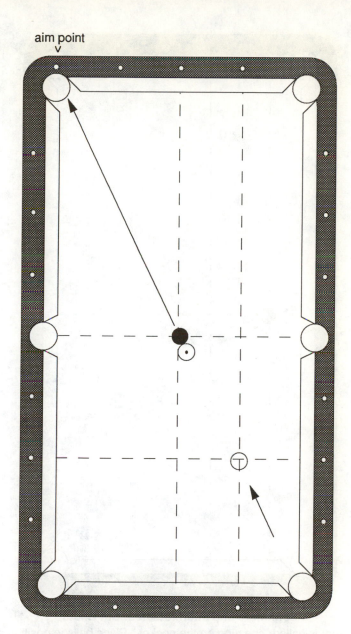

aim point

Beginners and Intermediates: Straight in shots

Place the balls in position as shown. Align the cue stick through the vertical center of the cue ball. Strike the cue ball below the horizontal center of the cue ball. Use a firm soft stroke and use force two. If a ball is straight in then you only have to aim the cue ball for the pocket and the object ball will automatically enter the pocket. Be extra careful not to raise the tip of the cue or your body when striking the cue ball below center. Object ball is hit full. VERIFIED.

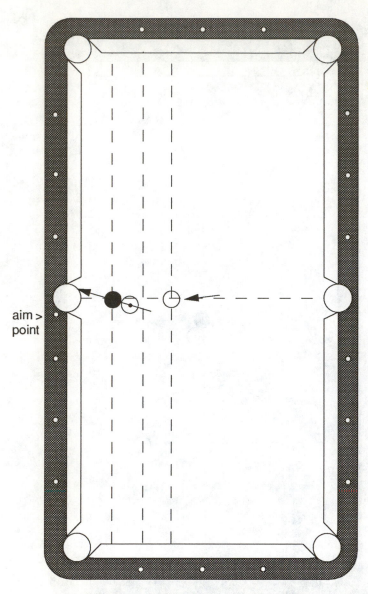

aim >
point

Beginners and Intermediates: Cut Shots

This shot is called "cheating on the pocket." Place balls in position as shown. Align the cue stick through the vertical center of the cue ball and in line with the aim point. Strike the cue ball below the horizontal center with a firm soft stroke using force one. This shot illustrates a system to avoid scratches while hitting the cue ball softly. Even though the ball is straight in, the ball may be cut in order to avoid a scratch of the cue ball or to play position for the next shot. Hold the cue level. Object ball is 5/8 cut. Verified.

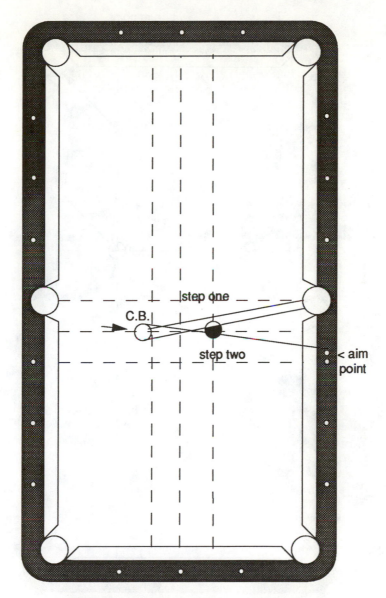

Beginners and Intermediates: Cut Shots

The angle of derivation equals the angle of adjustment

Place balls in position as shown. Examine the entry into the pocket of the cue ball. See what portion of the obstructing object ball is outside the viewing area. The next step is to reverse the angle so as to view the same amount of the object ball exposed on the opposite side. Strike the cue ball with a firm soft stroke. This shot sequence is only possible when the object ball obstructs the path of the cue ball for the pocket. Object ball is 1/2 cut. VERIFIED.

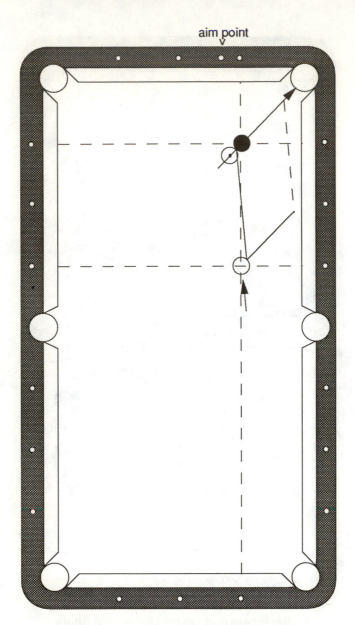

aim point

Beginners and Intermediates: Cut Shots

Place balls in position as shown. Align the cue stick through the center of the ball and in line with the aim point. Strike the cue ball above the horizontal dividing line and on the vertical center line. Employ a soft stroke using force two. Please note in the diagram the two diagonal lines; one representing the path of the object ball to the pocket and the other representing a parallel line drawn from the cue ball in a similar manner. A line is drawn between the two balls where the diagonals meet the balls. A parallel line is then made to determine the aim point. The shot pattern resembles a parallelogram. Object ball is 1/5 cut. Verified.

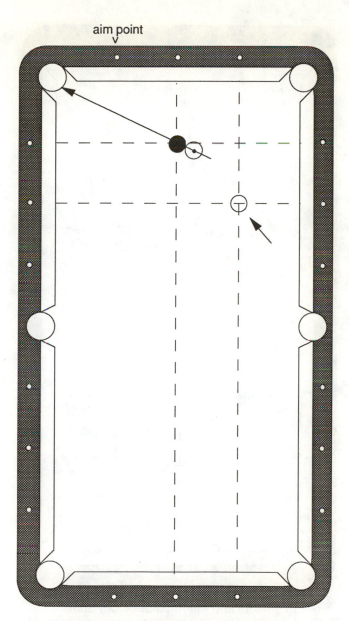

aim point

Beginners and Intermediates: Cut Shots

First check the ball entry into the pocket. Select the most favorable
entry. Next place a ball next to the object ball to represent a phantom
cue ball. Draw a line between the centers. Extend the line to the rail
and place a sighting object in place for an aim point. Remove the ball
representing the phantom cue ball. Strike the cue ball above the
horizontal center on the vertical line dividing the cue ball. Use a firm
stroke. use force one and one half. Hold the cue level. Object ball is
5/8 cut. Verified.

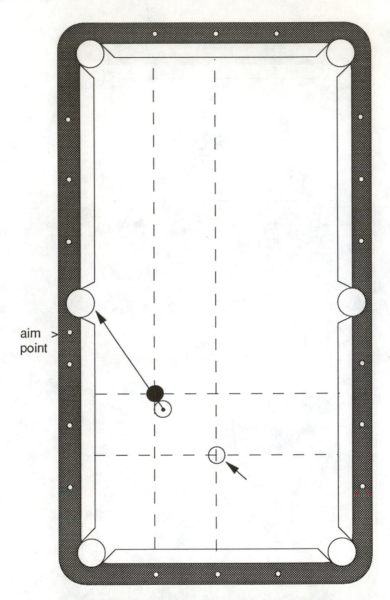

aim >
point

Beginners and Intermediates: Cut Shots

Place balls in position as shown. Check the entry of the object ball for the pocket. In this shot a ==consideration must be made to avoid the nearest corner of the pocket to the object ball.== Align the cue stick through the center of the cue ball and in line with the aim point on the rail. Strike the cue ball above the horizontal center and in line with the vertical axis. Use a firm soft stroke and force one. Hold the cue stick level and keep the hands in position until after the shot completion. Object ball is 5/8 cut. Verified.

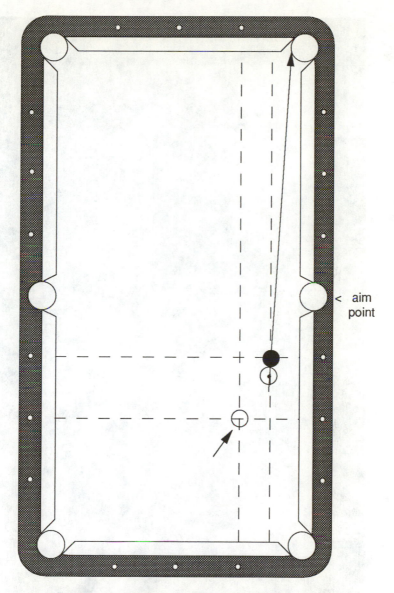

< aim
point

Beginners and Intermediates: Cut Shots

First check the entry into the pocket. You need to avoid striking the rail above the pocket opening. Striking the rail before the pocket opening could cause a miss. Also it could cause the ball to remain in the pocket or near the pocket which may be to your opponent's advantage. Align the cue stick through the center of the cue ball and in line with the aim point. Strike the cue ball below center with a moderate soft stroke using force two. Hold the cue level and only move your stroking arm during the shot. Object ball is 1/2 cut. Verified.

97

Beg. & Inter.-Cut Shots 43-C.Raftis-O.H.

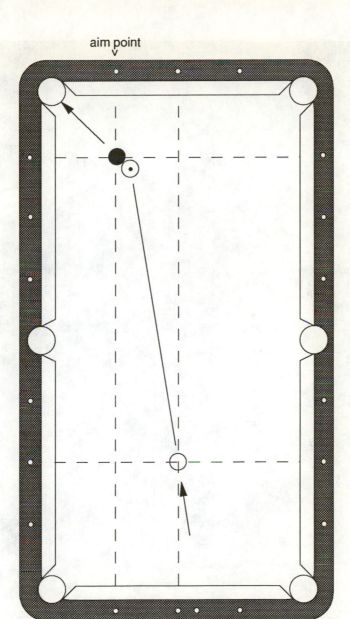

aim point

Beginners and Intermediates: Cut Shots

Place balls as shown. Check entry of object ball for pocket. Always select the most favorable entry. Next place a ball next to the desired object ball and in line with the pocket. This then is a phantom cue ball or the cue ball at the time of impact. Draw a line between the centers of the two cue balls. Extend the line to the rail and place a sighting aid at the end of the line. Now remove the ball representing the phantom cue ball. Align the cue stick through the center line of the cue ball and in line with the aim point. Strike the cue ball above the horizontal center and on the vertical axis line. Use a firm soft stroke and use force two. Object ball is 3/8 cut. Verified with photo.

Beg. & Intermediates-Cut Shots 40-K Ann-O.H.

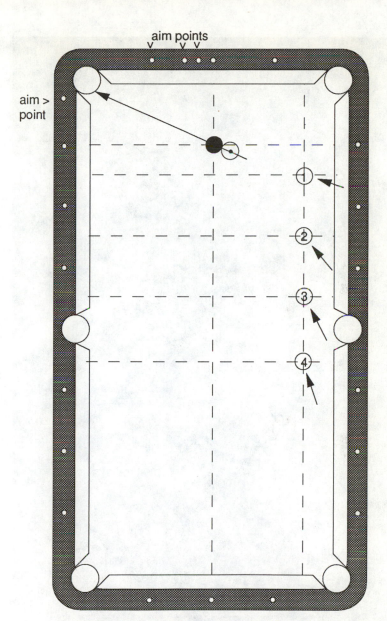

aim points

aim >
point

Beginners and Intermediates: Cut Shots

Position balls as shown. Align the cue stick through the center of the cue ball and in line with the aim point. Strike the cue ball above the horizontal center and on the vertical center line. Employ a firm soft stroke using force two and three. Hold the cue stick level and maintain your body posture until after the cue ball contacts the object ball. Always follow through the cue ball with the cue stick and make corrections to your stroke based upon the results experienced.1. O.B. 15/16 cut 2. O.B. 1/2 cut 3. O.B. 1/3 cut 4. O.B. 1/4 cut. Verified with photo.

101

Beg. & Intermediates-Cut Shots 53-K Ann-O.H.

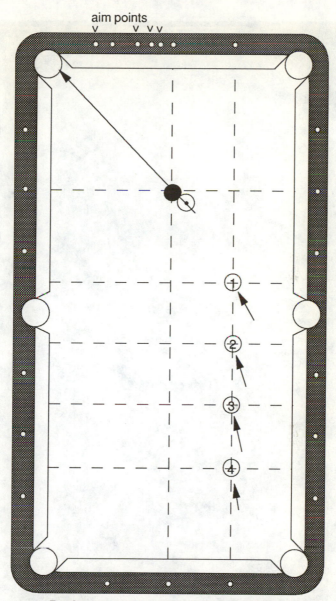

aim points

Beginners and Intermediates: Cut Shots

Position balls as shown. Align the cue stick through the center of the cue ball and in line with the aim point. Strike the cue ball below the horizontal center and on the vertical dividing line. Employ a firm moderate stroke using force three and four. Hold the cue stick level and maintain your body posture until after the cue ball contacts the object ball. Profit from your mistakes by examining the shot pattern after the execution. In order to do that you will have to maintain your follow through position until after impact. 1. O.B. 2/3 cut 2. O.B. 1/2 cut 3. O.B. 7/16 cut 4. O.B. 1/4 cut. Verified.

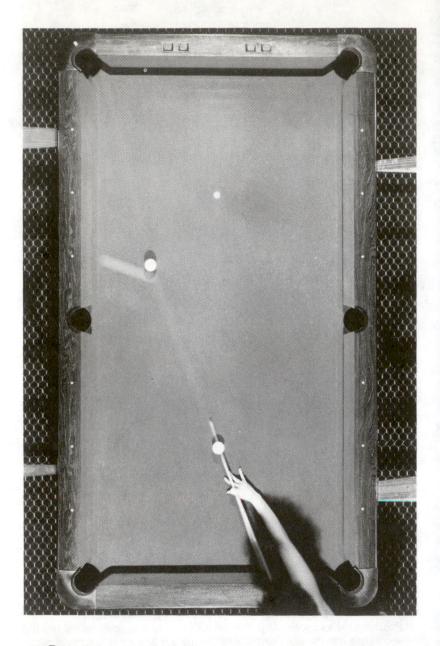

Beg. & Intermediates-Cut Shots 54-K Ann-O.H.

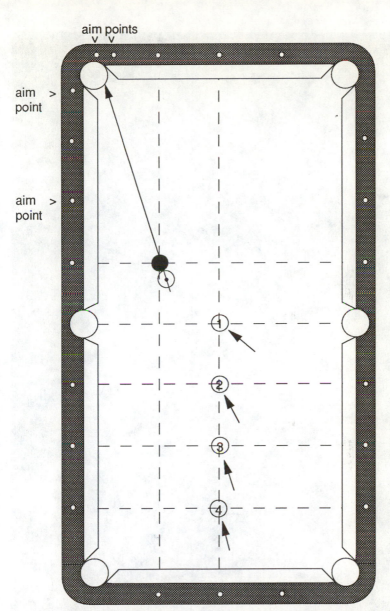

aim points
v v

aim >
point

aim >
point

Beginners and Intermediates: Cut Shots
Place balls in position as shown. Align the cue stick through the
center of the cue ball and in line with the aim point. Strike the cue ball
above the horizontal center and in line with the vertical center line.
Employ a firm moderate stroke using force three. Remember when
the cue ball and the object ball are in a line straight for a pocket, strike
the cue ball below center and follow through. 1. O.B. 1/2 cut 2. O.B.
3/4 cut 3. O.B. full hit 4. O.B. 7/8 cut. Verified with photo.

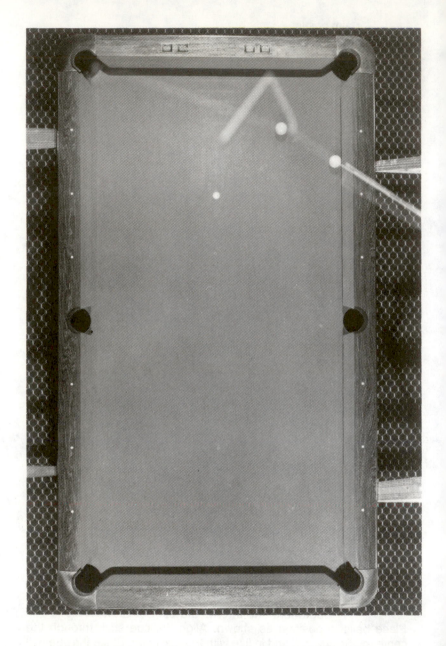

Beg. & Intermediates-Cut Shots 51-K Ann-O.H.

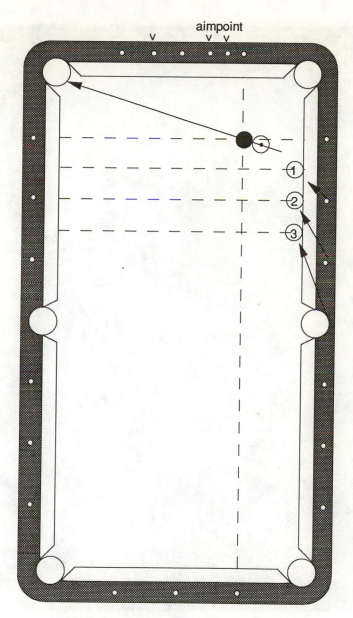

Beginners and Intermediates: Cut Shots

Place balls in position as shown. Align the cue stick through the center of the cue ball and in line with the aim point. Strike the cue ball above the horizontal center line and on the vertical dividing line. Employ a firm soft stroke using force two. 1. O.B. 1/2 cut 2. O.B. 1/4 cut 3. O.B. 1/5 cut. Verified with photo.

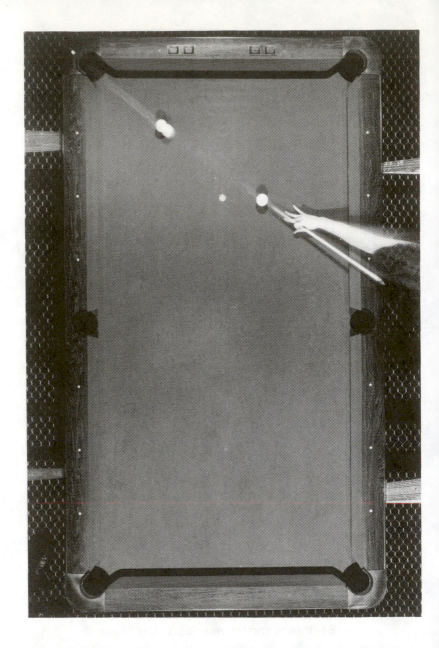

Beg. & Intermediates-Cut Shots 55-K Ann-O.H.

108

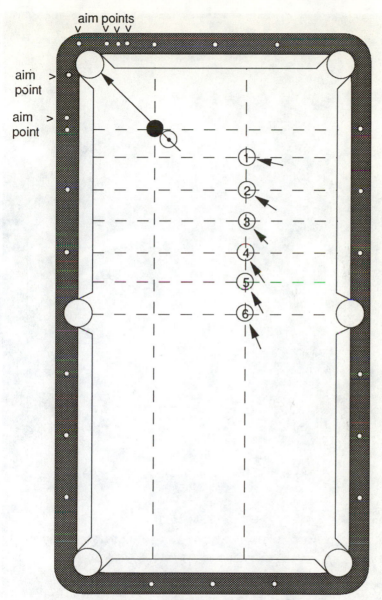

Beginners and Intermediates: Cut Shots

Place balls in position as shown. Align the cue stick through the center of the cue ball and in line with the aim point. Strike the cue ball at the junction of the vertical and horizontal dividing lines. Employ a firm soft stroke using force three and four. 1. O.B. 1/2 cut 2. O.B. 3/4 cut 3. O.B. full hit 4. O.B. 2/3 cut 5. O.B. 5/8 cut 6. O.B. 1/2 cut. Verified with photo.

Beg. & Intermediates-Cut Shots 41-K Ann-O.H.

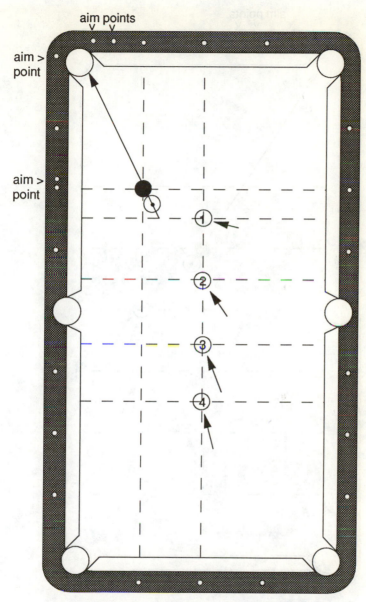

Beginners and Intermediates: Cut Shots

Place the balls in position as shown. Align the cue stick through the center of the cue ball and in line with the aim point. Strike the cue ball above the horizontal center and in line with the vertical center. Employ a firm soft stroke using force three. Remember when the cue ball and the object ball are in a line straight for a pocket, strike the cue ball below center and follow through. 1. O.B. 1/4 cut 2. O.B. 7/8 cut 3. O.B. 15/16 cut 4. O.B. 5/8 cut. Verified with photo.

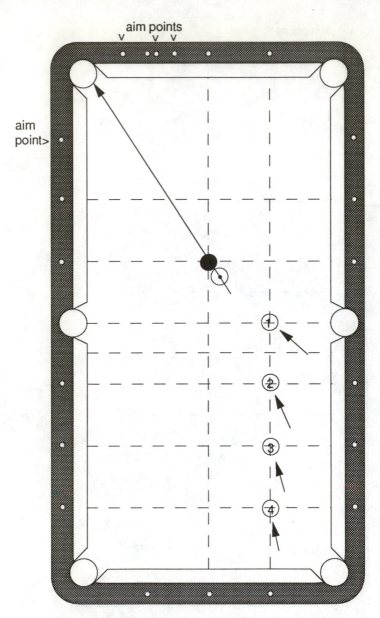

Beginners and Intermediates: Cut Shots

Position balls as shown. Align the cue stick through the center of the cue ball and in line with the aim point. Strike the cue ball above the horizontal center and on the vertical dividing line. Employ a firm moderate stroke using force four. Hold the cue stick level and maintain your body posture until after the cue ball contacts the rubber cushion. 1. O.B. 5/8 cut 2. O.B. 2/3 cut 3. O.B. 3/4 cut 4. O.B. 1/2 cut. Verified.

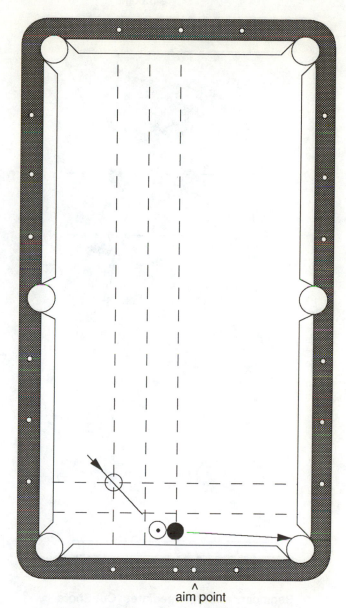

^
aim point

Beginners and Intermediates: Cut Shot

Position balls as shown. Notice that the object ball is approximately one inch from the rubber cushion. Align the cue stick through the center of the cue ball and in line with the aim point. Strike the cue ball above the horizontal center and in line with the vertical dividing line. Employ a firm soft stroke using force two. So when the object ball is near a rubber cushion we aim the cue stick at a point half way between the edge of the object ball and the cushion; thereby striking the object ball and the cushion at the same time. Object ball is 1/4 cut. Verified.

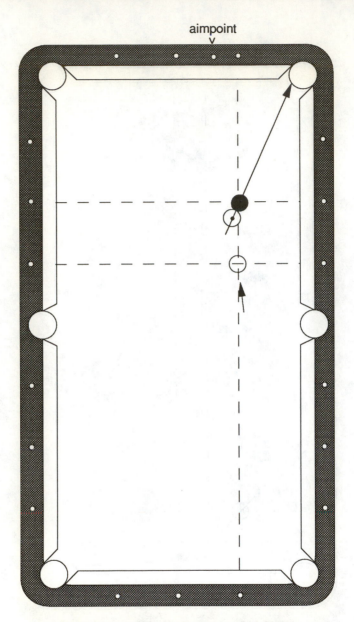

aimpoint
∨

Beginners and Intermediates: Cut Shots

First check the ball entry into the pocket. Select the most favorable entry. Next place the a ball next to the object ball to represent a phantom cue ball. Draw a line through the centers of the two cue ball and place a sighting aid on the rail at the end of the line. Now remove the ball representing the phantom cue ball. Strike the cue ball below the horizontal center and in line with the vertical center. Use a firm stroke. Use force number two. Avoid a high hit cue ball hard and a center hit cue ball medium as those hits might bring the cue ball into pocket number four causing a scratch or loss of shot. Object ball is 1/2 cut. Verified.

114

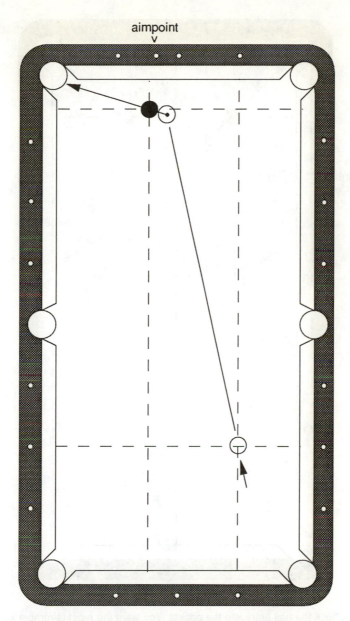

aimpoint
v

Beginners and Intermediates: Cut Shots

First check the ball entry into the pocket. Select the most favorable entry.
Next place the a ball next to the object ball to represent a phantom cue ball.
Now draw a line through the centers of the two cue balls and place a sighting
device on the rail. Now remove the ball representing the phantom cue ball.
Align the cue tip through the center line of the horizontal center and on the
vertical axis line. Use a firm soft stroke and force number two. Object ball is
1/5 cut. Verified.

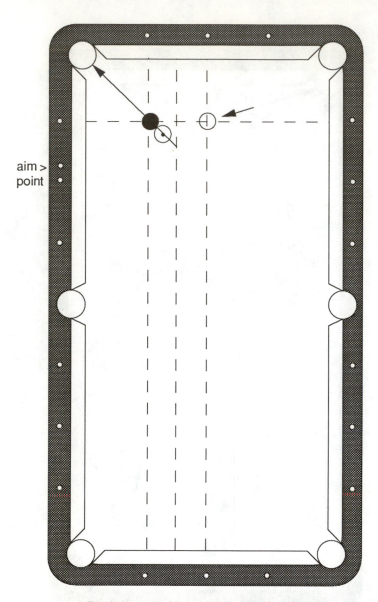

aim >
point

Beginners and Intermediates: Cut Shots

First check the ball entry into the pocket. You want the most favorable entry; i.e. with the least chance of missing. Next place another ball next to the object ball. This ball represents the cue ball when it is in contact with the object ball; in other words it is a phantom cue ball. Align the cue stick through the center of the cue ball and the aim point. The aim point was determined by extending a line through the centers of the cue ball and the phantom cue ball. Strike the cue ball above the horizontal center using a soft stroke or force number one and one half. Remember after finding the aim point, remove the ball that represents the phantom cue ball. Object ball is 1/5 cut. Verified.

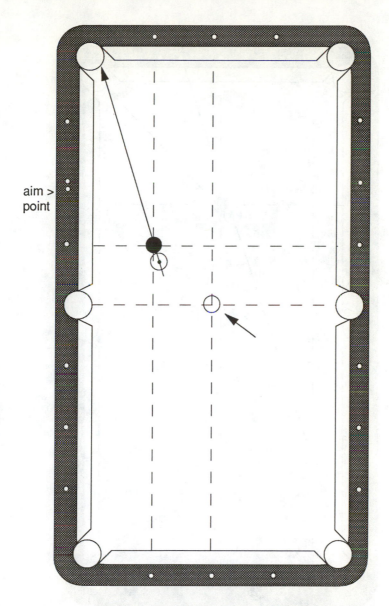

aim >
point

Beginners and Intermediates: Cut Shots

First check the ball entry into the pocket. Select the most favorable entry. Next place a ball next to the object ball to represent a phantom cue ball. Draw a line through the centers of the two cue balls and place a sighting aid on the rail at the end of the line. Now remove the ball representing the phantom cue ball. Strike the cue ball above the horizontal center and on the line of the vertical center. Use a firm soft stroke. Use force number two. Hold the cue level and at the impact let the tip of the cue travel in an upward motion. Object ball is 7/16 cut. Verified

117

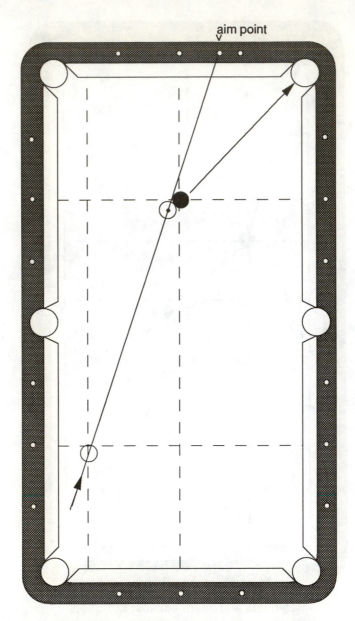

aim point

Beginners and Intermediates: The Cut Shot

Place the balls in position as shown. Align the cue stick through the center of the cue ball and in line with the aim point. Strike the cue ball above the horizontal line and slightly to the left of the vertical dividing line. Employ a firm soft stroke using force four. This is also an illustration of how to use the billiard protractor to determine the hit point which in this case is 150° or a half ball hit. Object ball is a 1/2 cut. VERIFIED.

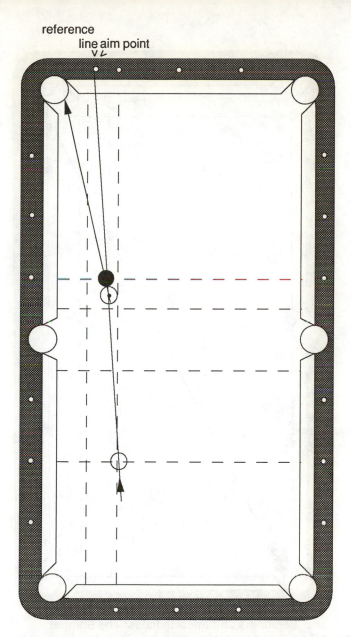

reference line aim point

Beginners and Intermediates: The Cut Shot

Place the balls in position as shown. Examine the shot pattern. Look at the position of the object ball and the cue ball along the reference line with the desired entry into the pocket. After noticing the amount of deviation, align the cue stick through the center of the cue ball and in line with the aim point. Strike the cue ball above the horizontal center and in line with the vertical center using force four. employ a firm moderate stroke. The line is drawn between the centers of the two balls. Object ball is 7/8 cut. VERIFIED.

119

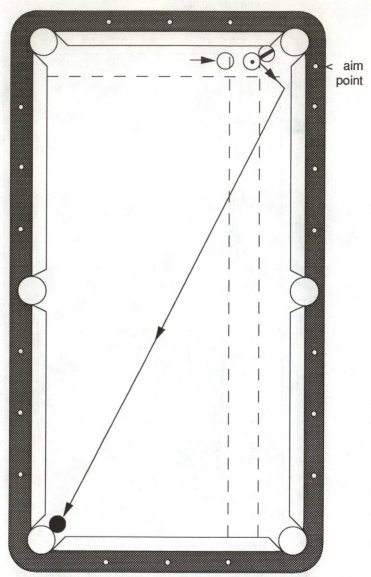

< aim
point

Beginners and Intermediates: The Spinner

Position the balls on the table as shown. Align the cue stick through the center of the cue ball and in line with the aim point. Parallel the line of aim in order to strike the cue ball one cue tip below the horizontal center and one and one half cue tips to the right of the vertical center. Employ a firm moderate stroke using force six. Object ball is 1/4 cut. Verified.

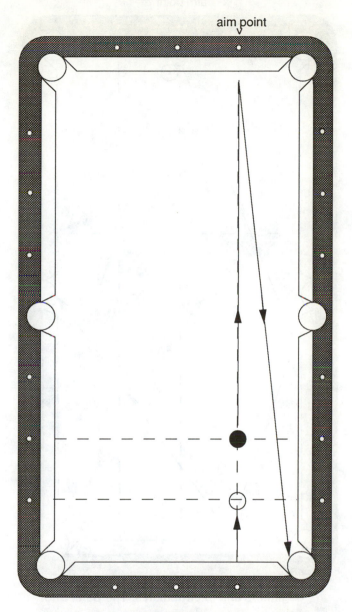

aim point

Beginners and Intermediates: The Bank Shot

Place the balls in position as shown. Align the cue stick through the center of the cue ball and in line with the aim point. Now parallel the line of aim by moving the cue stick to the left of the vertical center and on the horizontal center line. Move the cue stick about two and one half cue tips to the left of center or about three fourths of an inch. Strike the cue ball with a moderate stroke employing force five. This shot pattern illustrates the transference of english from the cue ball to the object ball. Object ball is hit full. Verified.

121

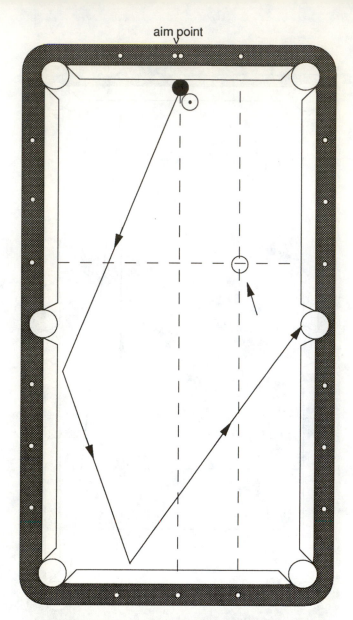

aim point

Beginners and Intermediates: The Bank Shot

Place the balls in position as shown. Align the cue stick through the center of the cue ball and in line with the aim point. Now parallel the line of aim in order to strike the cue ball to the left of the vertical center line and below the horizontal center line. Strike the cue ball with a moderate stroke using force five. Due to the strong speed you do not have to allow for the influence of the off center hit on the cue ball. the shot is played in this manner to avoid a kiss or a double contact of the cue ball with the object ball. Object ball is 5/8 cut. Verfied. Shot depends on skill level.

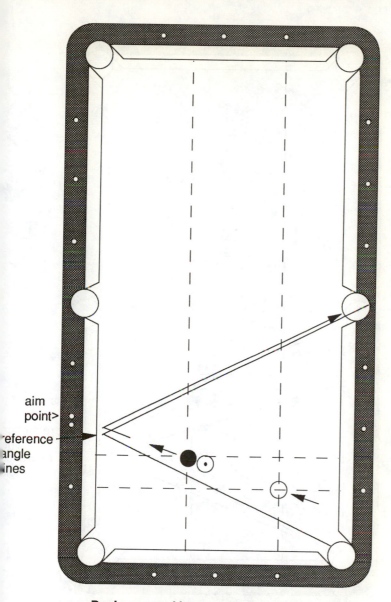

aim
point>

reference
angle
lines

Beginners and Intermediates: The Bank Shot

Place the balls in position as shown. We are using for a reference an
equal angle produced by dividing an equal distance and surface area
in half. By paralleling the reference line we create an equal angle for
the bank shot. Align the cue stick through the center of the cue ball and
parallel to the reference line. Strike the cue ball at the junction of the
horizontal and vertical dividing lines. Use a moderate soft stroke and
employ force three. Hold the cue level and do not change your body
position until after the shot has been executed. Object ball is full.hit.
VERIFIED.

123

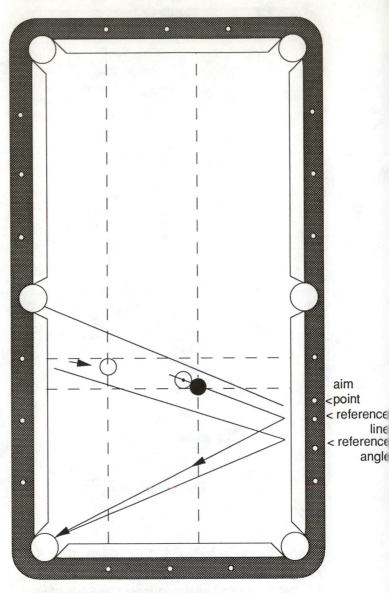

aim
<point
< reference
line
< reference
angle

Beginners and Intermediates: The Bank Shot
one rail across the corner

Position the balls as shown. Align the cue stick through the center of the cue ball and in line with the aim point. Strike the cue ball in the center at the junction of the vertical and horizontal dividing lines. Strike the cue ball with a firm soft stroke using force three. Hold the cue level and leave the cue stick on the table after striking the cue ball. By using reference lines we are able to interpret the hit point on the rubber cushion; after which we are able to determine the aim point on the rail. Object ball is 5/8 cut. VERIFIED.

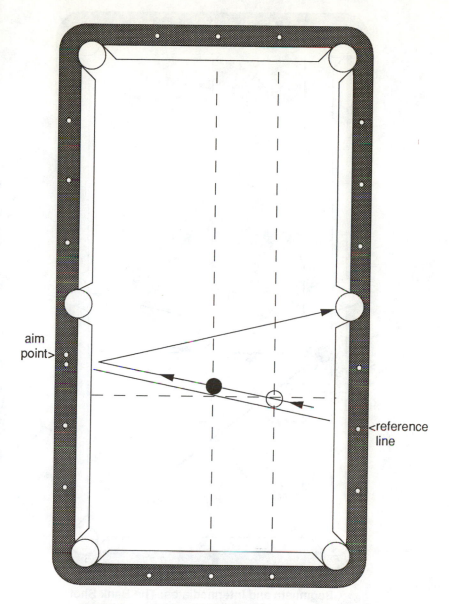

aim
point>

<reference
line

Beginners and Intermediates: The Bank Shot

Place the balls in position as shown. Align the cue stick through the center of the cue ball and in line with the aim point. Strike the cue ball on the vertical center line and above the the horizontal dividing line. employ a firm moderate stroke using force five. In this diagram the balls are located on a parallel line next to the refrerence line. So in order to make the shot we have a choice. Either to cut the object ball to the left into the rail and play a slow bounce off the cushion or play the ball straight on and overstroke the shot or in other words strike the cue ball harder than necessary in order to shorten the rebound angle. Object ball is hit full. VERIFIED.

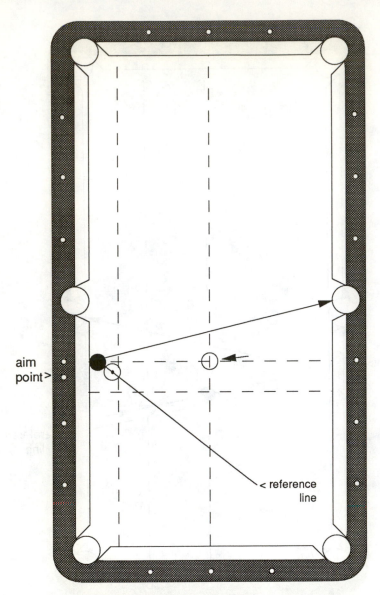

aim
point >

< reference
line

Beginners and Intermediates: The Bank Shot

Place the balls in position as shown. In order to avoid the cue ball striking the object ball twice and spoiling the shot you play an overcut on the object ball and reverse english on the cue ball. Note the reference line for the overcut. Align the cue stick with the center line of the cue ball and the aim point. Parallel this alignment and adjust the aim point for striking the cue ball right of the vertical center and below the horizontal line. Strike the cue ball with a firm moderate stroke using force three. Object ball is 1/4 cut. VERIFIED. Elevate cue 10°

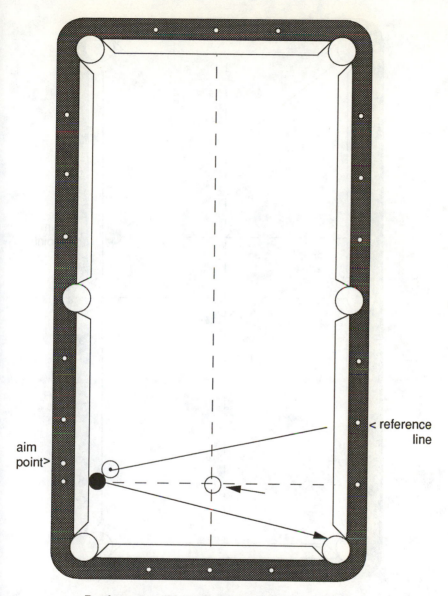

aim
point>

< reference
line

Beginners and Intermediates: The Bank Shot

Place the balls in position. Align the cue stick through the center of the cue ball and in line with the aim point. Now parellel the line to strike the cue ball below the horizontal dividing line and to the left of the vertical dividing line. Strike the cue ball with a firm soft stroke using force three. By drawing a line between the phantom cue ball and the object ball you will notice that we are overcutting the object ball and using reverse english on the cue ball in order to hold the object ball into the short angle. The shot is played in this manner in order to avoid the cue ball striking the object ball twice. Object ball is 1/4 cut. VERIFIED.

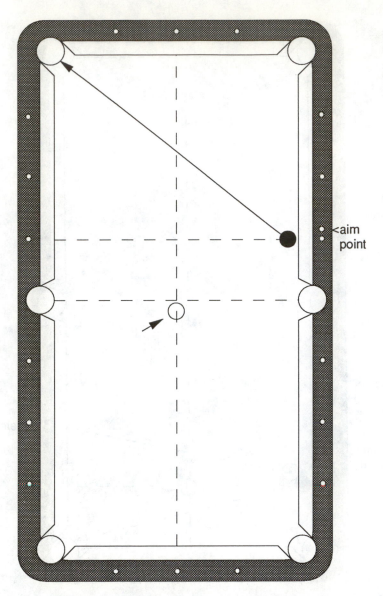

aim point

Beginners and Intermediates: The Bank Shot

Place the balls in position as shown. Align the cue stick through the center of the cue ball and in line with the aim point. Parallel the line of aim in order to strike the cue ball one and one half cue tips below the horizontal dividing line and one half of a cue tip to the right of the vertical dividing line. Employ a firm moderate stroke using force five. Object ball is 3/4 cut. VERIFIED.

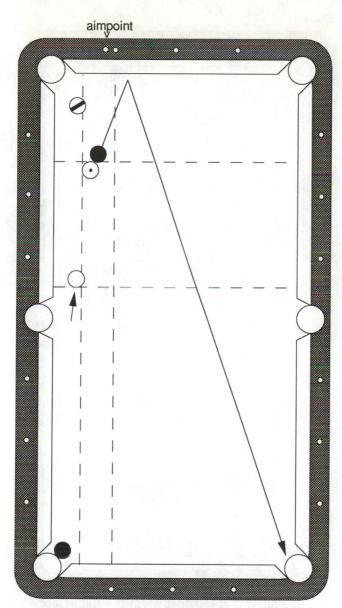

Advanced & Expert: The Bank Shot

Place the balls in position as shown. Align the cue stick through the center of the cue ball and in line with the aim point. Parallel that line of aim in order to strike the cue ball slightly above the horizontal line and one and one half cue tips to the left of the vertical dividing line. Employ a firm moderate stroke using force five. Object ball is 1/2 cut. Verified.

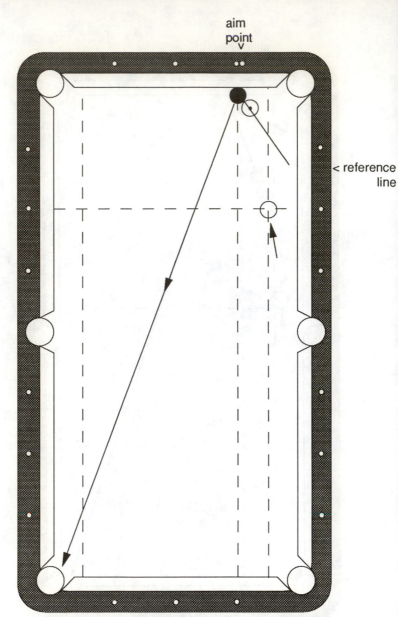

aim
point
v

< reference
line

Beginners and Intermediates: The Bank Shot

Position balls in position as shown. Align the cue stick through the center of the cue ball and in line with the aim point. Strike the cue ball to the left of the vertical center and below the horizontal center by paralleling the cue stick to the left of the original line of aim. The objective on this shot pattern is to overcut the object ball and then english the cue ball with reverse english in order to hold the object ball or pull the object ball into line. Playing the shot in this manner is necessary in order to avoid a kiss or double hit of the cue ball with the object ball. Object ball is 1/2 cut. Verified.

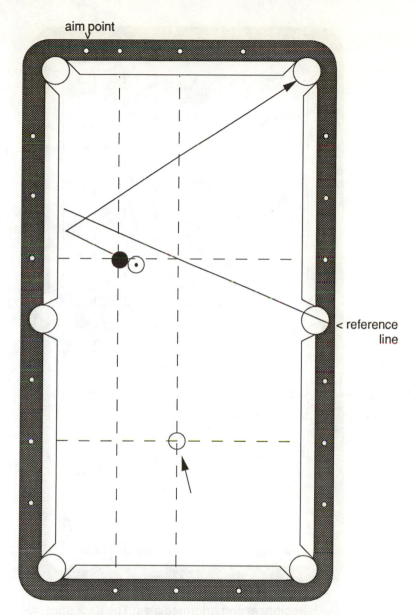

Beginners and Intermediates: The Bank Shot

Place balls in position as shown. Align the cue stick through the center of the cue ball and in line with the aim point. Now parallel the line of aim in order to strike the cue ball two cue tips or one half inch to the left of the vertical center line. In the line up of the cue allow two degrees for the throw of the center hit. Use a moderate firm stroke and force four. The shot is played in this manner in order to avoid a kiss or a double contact with the cue ball. Similar shot patterns come up during games. Object ball is 1/5 cut. Verified.

131

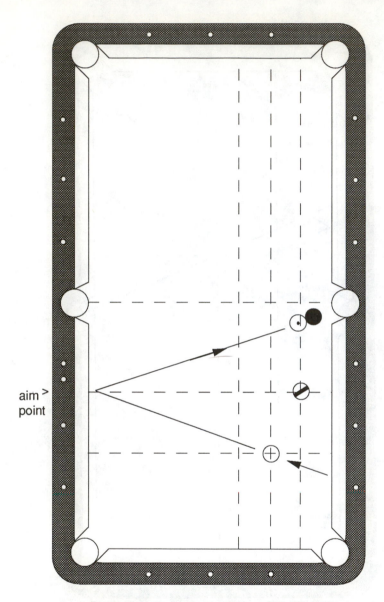

aim >
point

Beginners and Intermediates: The Kick Shot

Place the balls in position as shown. Align the cue stick through the center of the cue ball and in line with the aim point. Strike the cue ball at the conjunction or meeting place of the horizontal and vertical dividing lines. Use a soft firm stroke employing force three. Hold the cue level. Only allow the stroking arm to move. Do not move your body position or the cue alignment until after the shot is well on its way to completion. The cue ball will turn over after contact with the rail. In other words the cue ball will have a forward roll both before and after striking the cushion. Object ball is hit full. VERIFIED.

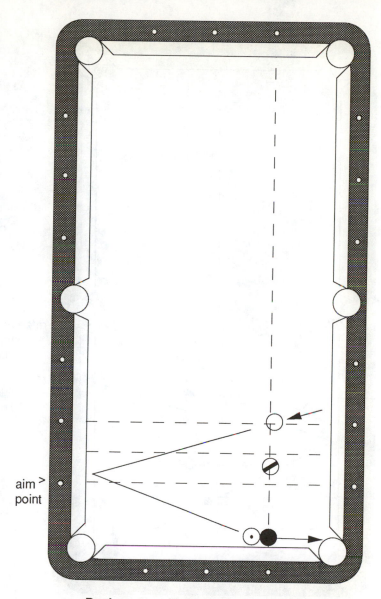

aim >
point

Beginners and Intermediates: The Kick Shot

Place the balls in position as shown. Here we have divided the distance between the cue ball and the object ball in order to create an equal angle. Align the cue stick through the vertical center of the cue ball and in line with the aim point. Strike the cue ball one half a cue tip above the horizontal center line or one quarter of an inch above the horizontal center line. Use a firm soft stroke and employ force three. Hold the cue stick level. Avoid moving the position of the body until after the cue ball has contacted the rail. Object ball is 1/2 hit. VERIFIED.

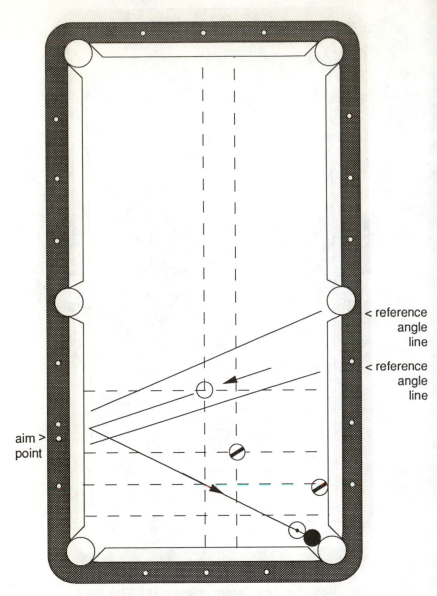

< reference
angle
line

< reference
angle
line

aim >
point

Beginners and Intermediates: The Kick Shot

Place the balls in position as shown. By knowing the reference lines from the angle of incidence equals the angle of reflection, you may make an interpretation such as the shot illustrated. Align the cue stick through the vertical and horizontal center of the cue ball and in line with the aim point. Strike the cue ball with a firm soft stroke using force two. In order to avoid scratching or in other words to avoid the cue ball following in behind the object ball the right speed is very important. Object ball is full hit. Verified.

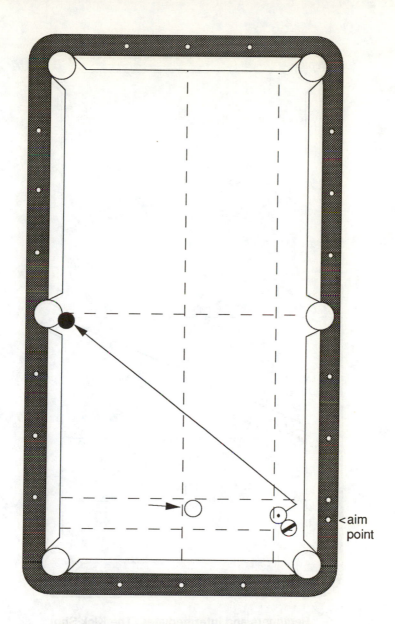

<aim
point

Beginners and Intermediates: The Kick Shot

Place the balls in position as shown. Align the cue stick through the
center of the cue ball and in line with the aim point. Parallel that line of
aim in order to strike the cue ball one cue tip below the horizontal line
and and one cue tip to the left of the vertical dividing line. Employ a
firm moderate stroke using force five. Object ball is 1/2 cut. Verified.

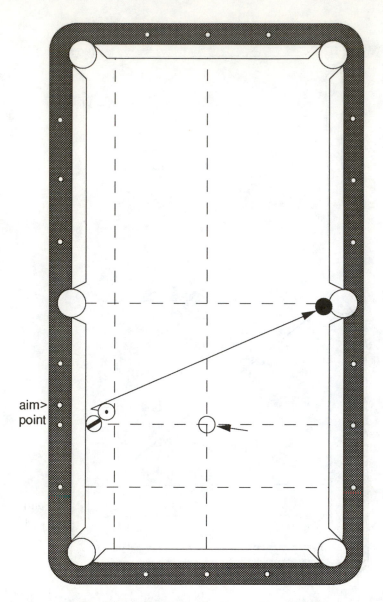

aim>
point

Beginners and Intermediates: The Kick Shot

Place the balls in position as shown. Align the cue stick through the center of the ball and in line with the aim point. Parallel the line of aim in order to strike the cue ball one half of a cue tip below the horizontal center and one cue tip to the left of the vertical dividing line. Strike the cue ball with a firm soft stroke using force three. Object ball is 1/ 16 cut. Verified.

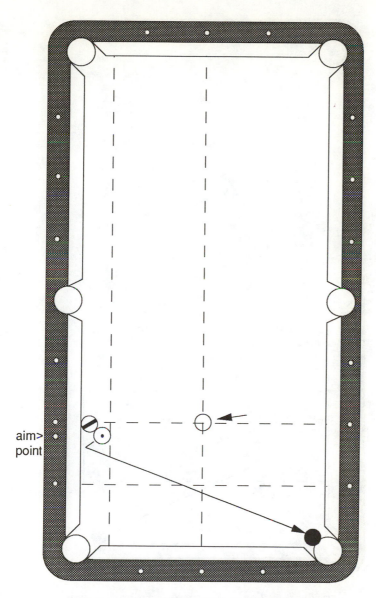

aim>
point

Beginners and Intermediates: The Kick Shot

Place the balls in position as shown. Align the cue stick through the center of the ball and in line with the aim point. Parallel the line of aim in order to strike the cue ball one half of a cue tip below center and one cue tip to the right of the vertical dividing line. Strike the cue ball with a firm soft stroke using force four. Object ball is 1/8 cut. Verified.

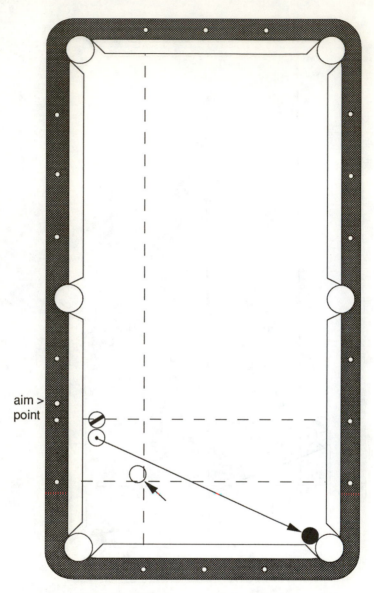

aim >
point

Beginners and Intermediates: The Draw Kick

Place the balls in position as shown. Align the cue stick through the
center of the cue ball and in line with the aim point. Parallel that line of
aim in order to strike the cue ball one cue tip below the horizontal line
and one half of a cue tip to the left of the vertical dividing line. Employ
a firm moderate stroke using force five. Object ball is full hit. 1/4 cut.
Verified.

138

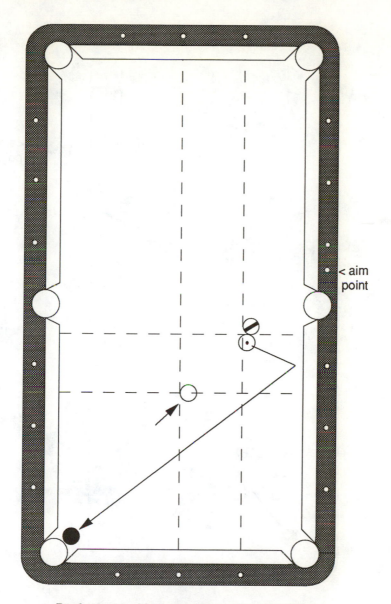

< aim
point

Beginners and Intermediates: The Kick Shot

Place the balls in position as shown. Align the cue stick through the center of the ball and in line with the aim point. Parallel that line of aim in order to strike the cue ball one cue tip below the horizontal line and one cue tip to the right of the vertical dividing line. Strike the cue ball with a firm moderate stroke using force five. Object ball is 1/2 cut. VERIFIED.

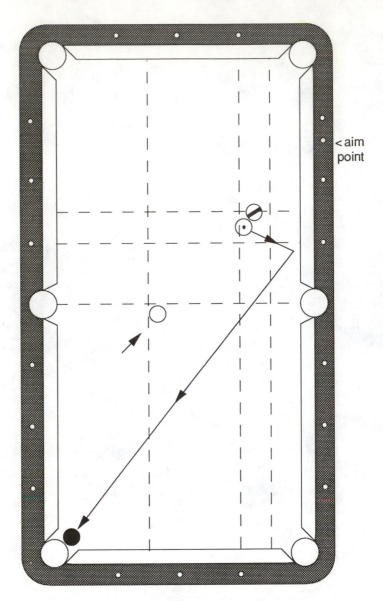

Beginners and Intermediates: The Kick Shot

Place the balls in position as shown. Align the cue stick through the center of the ball and in line with the aim point. Parallel that line of aim in order to strike the cue ball one cue tip below the horizontal dividing line and one cue tip to the right of the vertical dividing line. Strike the cue ball with a firm moderate stroke using force five. Object ball is 3/4 cut. VERIFIED.

140

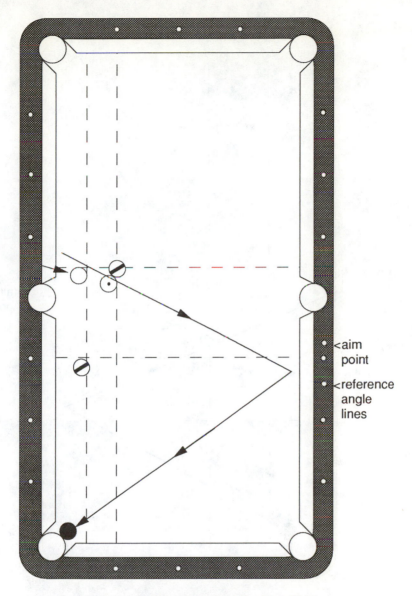

<aim
point

<reference
angle
lines

Beginners and Intermediates: The Kick Shot

Place the balls in position as shown. Align the cue stick through the
center of the cue ball and in line with the aim point. Strike the cue ball
above the horizontal line. Strike the cue ball with a firm soft stroke
using force four. Object ball is 1/32 cut. VERIFIED

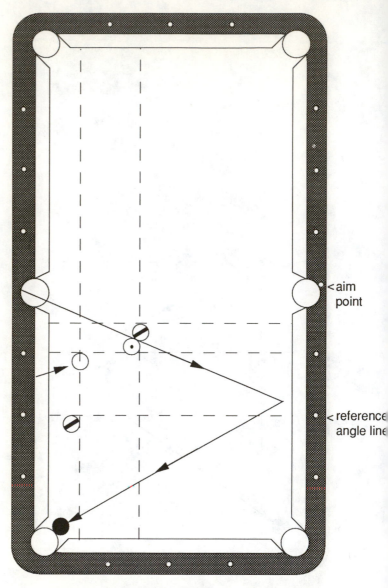

Beginners and Intermediates: The Kick Shot

Place the balls in position as shown. Align the cue stick through the center of the cue ball and in line with the aim point. Strike the cue ball at the junction of the horizontal and vertical dividing lines. Employ a firm soft stroke using force four. Object ball is 1/4 cut. VERIFIEID

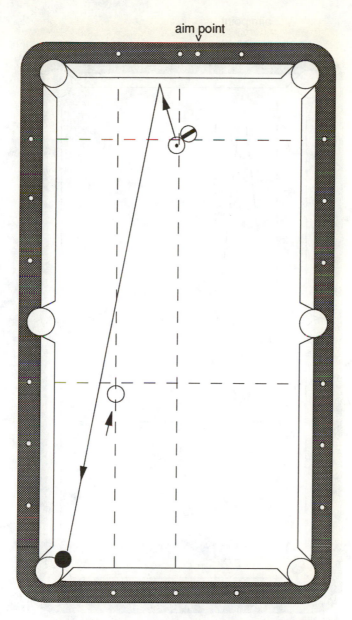

aim point

Beginners and Intermediates: The Kick Shot

Place the balls in position as shown. Align the cue stick through the center of the ball and in line with the aim point. Parallel the line of aim in order to strike the cue ball slightly above the horizontal center and one cue tip to the right of the vertical dividing line. Employ a firm moderate stroke using force five. Object ball is 1/2 cut. Verified. Elevate cue 10°

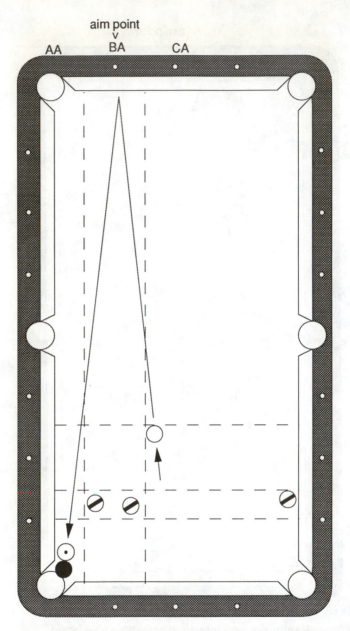

aim point
v
AA   BA   CA

Beginners and Intermediates: The Kick Shot

Position balls as shown. Align the cue stick through the center of the cue ball and in line with the aim point. Strike the cue ball with a firm moderate stroke using force five. Hold the cue level and maintain the body and head position until after the cue has contacted the rail cushion. Here we are using the reference angle from the angle of incidence equals the angle of reflection. Or in other words we have divided the distance on the rail between AA and CA in order to find the aim point at BA. Object ball is hit full. VERIFIED.

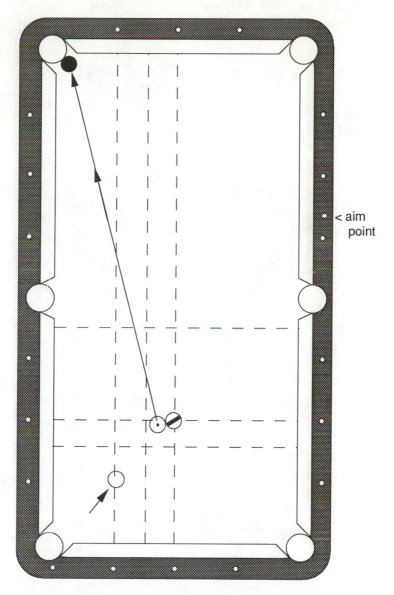

< aim
point

Advanced and Expert: The Dead Ball

Place the balls in position as shown. Align the cue stick through the center of the cue ball and in line with the aim point. Strike the cue ball slightly below the horizontal reference line one and one half cue tips. Employ a firm moderate stroke using force six. Verified.

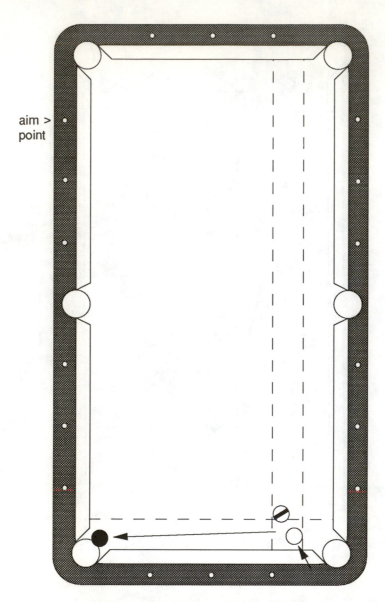

aim >
point

Beginners and Intermediates: The Kick Shot

Place the balls in position as shown. Align the cue stick through the center of the cue ball and in line with the aim point. Strike the cue ball one half cue tip below the horizontal dividing line and on the vertical dividing line. Strike the cue ball with firm soft stroke using force four. Object ball is 15/16 cut. Verified.

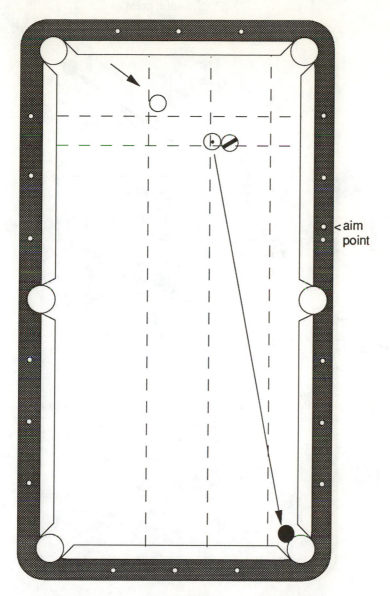

<aim
point

Beginners and Intermediates: The Kick Shot

Place the balls in position as shown. Align the cue stick through the center of the cue ball and in line with the aim point. Strike the cue ball one cue tip above the horizontal dividing line and on the vertical dividing line. Employ a firm moderate stroke using force five. The cue ball should swerve slightly before pocketing the desired object ball Object ball is 3/4 cut. Verified.

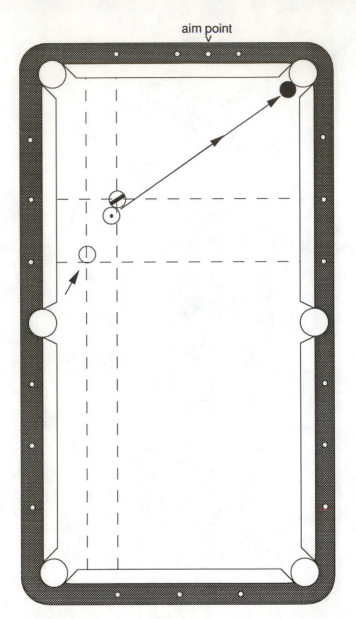

aim point

Beginners and Intermediates: The Kick Shot

Place the balls in position as shown. Align the cue stick through the center of the cue ball and in line with the aim point. Strike the cue ball one cue tip above the horizontal dividing line and on the vertical dividing line. Employ a firm moderate stroke using force four. Object ball is 7/8 cut. Verified.

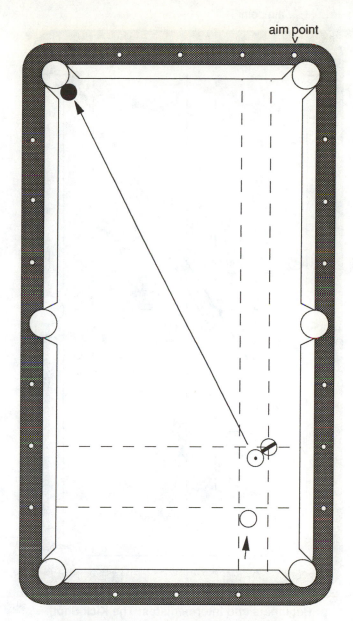

aim point

Beginners and Intermediates: The Kick Shot

Place the balls in position as shown. Align the cue stick through the center of the cue ball and in line with the aim point. Strike the cue ball above the horizontal dividing lines. Strike the cue ball with a firm soft stroke using force four. Object ball is 1/2 cut. Verified.

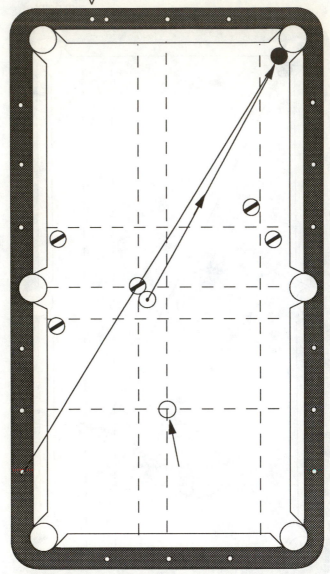

aimpoint

Beginners and Intermediates: The Kick Shot

Place balls in position as shown. Align the cue stick through the center
of the cue ball and in line with the aim point. Strike the cue ball above
the center by one cue tip, or one half inch and on the vertical dividing
line. Employ a firm soft stroke using force four. The diagram shows a
line drawn from the center of the object ball to the surface of an
obstructing ball. This then is alignment point for establishing the aim
point located on the rail. Hold the cue level and strike the cue ball in a
fluid rising motion. This shot will test your striking ability. Object ball is
3/4 cut. VERIFIED.

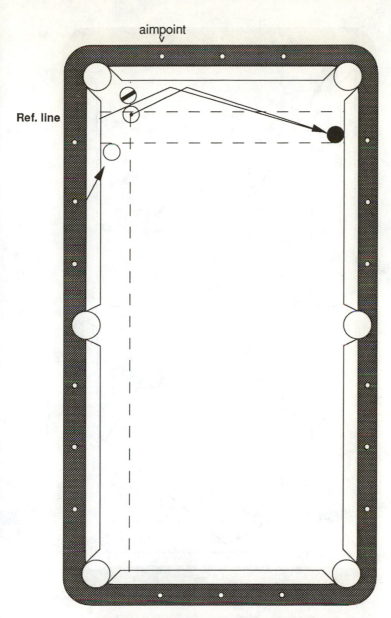

aimpoint

Ref. line

Beginners and Intermediates: The Kick Shot

Place balls in position as shown. Align the cue stick through the center of the cue ball and in line with the aim point. Strike the cue ball in the center at the junction of the vertical and horizontal dividing lines. Strike the cue ball with a firm soft stroke using force two. This shot can be used for playing a safety or a variation could be a two rails in the side pocket. Object ball is 1/2 cut. VERIFIED.

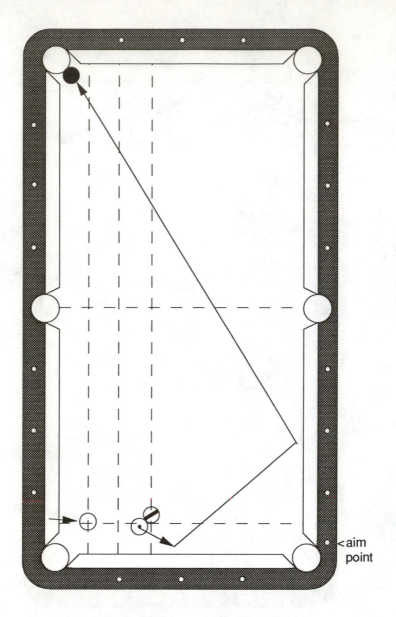

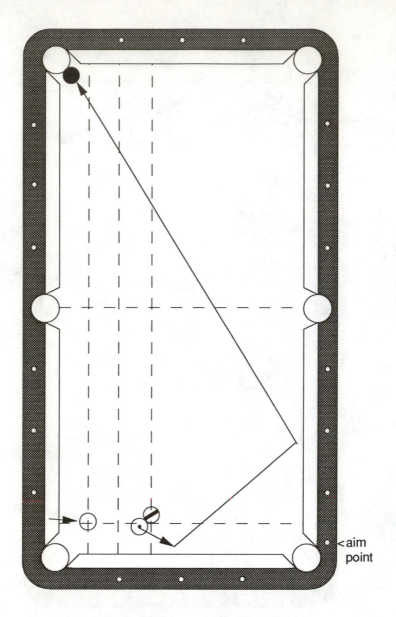

<aim
point

Beginners and Intermediates: The Kick Shot
Two Rails into the Corner

Place the balls in poition as shown. Align the cue stick throught the center of the cue ball and in line with the aim point. Parallel that line of aim in order to strike the cue ball slightly lower than one cue tip below the horizontal center and one half of a cue tip to the left of the vertical center. Strike the cue ball with a firm soft stroke using force four. Object ball is 1/2 cut. Verified.

152

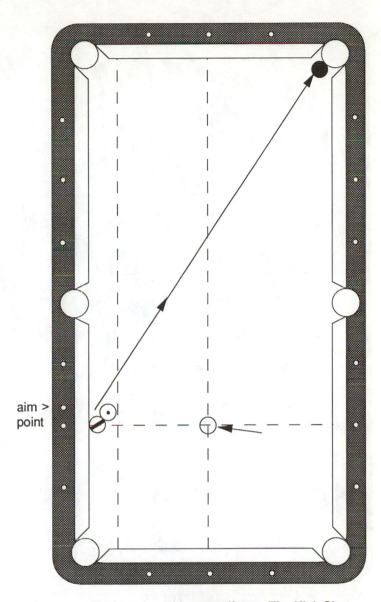

aim >
point

Beginners and Intermediates: The Kick Shot

Place the balls in position as shown. Align the cue stick through the center of the cue ball and in line with the aim point. Parallel that line of aim in order to strike the cue ball one cue tip below center and one half a cue tip to the right of the vertical dividing line. Strike the cue ball with a firm soft stroke using force four. Object ball is 1/4 cut. Verified.

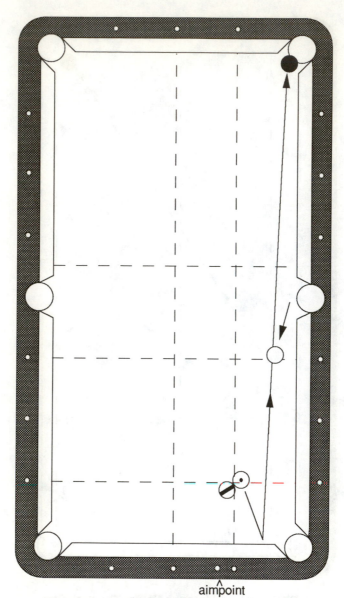

Beginners & Intermediate: The Kick Shot

Place the balls in position as shown. Align the cue stick through the center of the cue ball and in line with the aim point. Parallel that line of aim in order to strike the cue ball slightly above the horizontal dividing line and one and one half cue tips to the right of the vertical dividing line. Employ a firm moderate stroke using force five. Object ball is 1/2 cut. Verified.

154

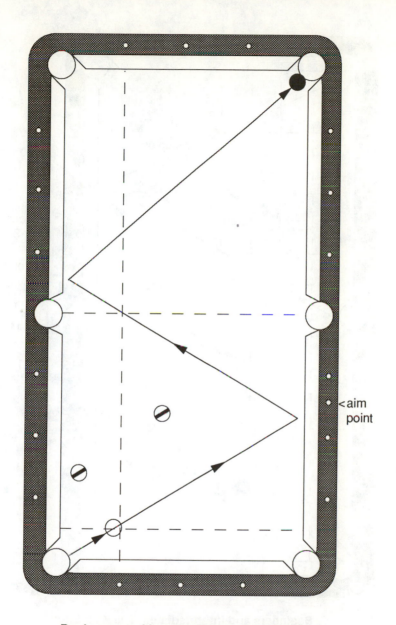

<aim
point

Beginners and Intermediates: The Kick Shot
Two Rails into the Corner

Diagrammed is a ball track for kick or bank shots into the corner. Strike the cue ball in the center and at the junction of the horizontal and vertical dividing lines. Employ a firm moderate stroke using force four. Hold the cue level and maintain body posture until the ball has struck the second rubber cushion. Object ball is hit full. Verified.

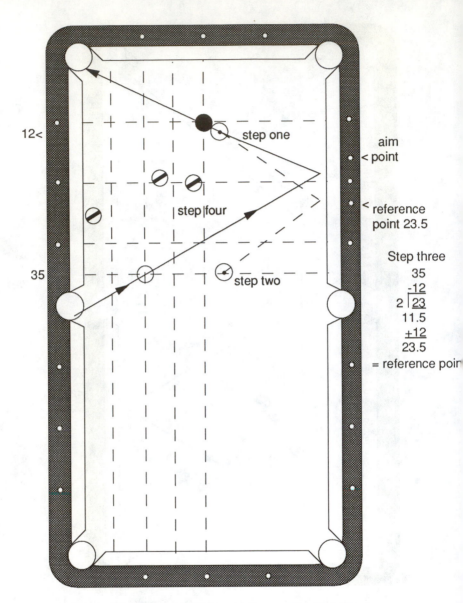

Beginners and Intermediates: The Kick Shot

Place balls in position as shown. Strike the cue ball in the center at the junction of the vertical and horizontal dividing lines. Use a firm easy stroke and force four. Hold the cue level and make a short follow through. In the diagram I have used two phantom cue balls. The distance between the two cue balls has been computed and a reference point has been found. The line from the actual cue ball is an interpretation. There are four steps to be followed to arrive at the aim point. Object ball is 2/3 cut. Verified.

156

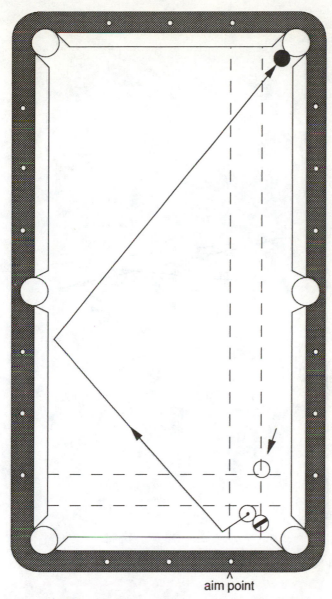

aim point

Beginners and Intermediates: The Kick Shot

Place the balls in position as shown. Align the cue stick through the center of the cue ball and in line with the aim point. Parallel that line of aim in order to strike the cue ball one half of a cue tip below the horizontal line and one half of a cue tip to the right of the vertical dividing line. Employ a firm moderate stroke using force four. Object ball is 1/8 cut. Verified.

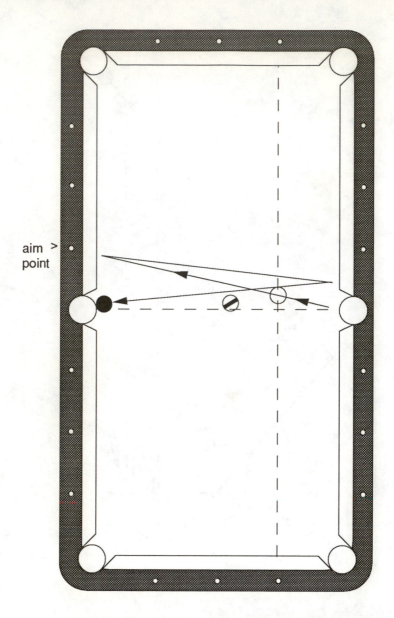

aim >
point

Beginners and Intermediates: The Kick Shot

Place the balls in position as shown. Align the cue stick through the center of
the cue ball and in line with the aim point. Now parallel the line of aim in order
to strike the cue ball below the horizontal center and to the left of the vertical
center line. Employ a firm moderate stroke using force six. Hold the cue level
and maintain your position until the cue ball has contacted the rubber cushion.
This shot pattern could be very important and valuable in producing a double
bank shot or to hit out of a difficult snooker. Object ball is hit full. Verified.

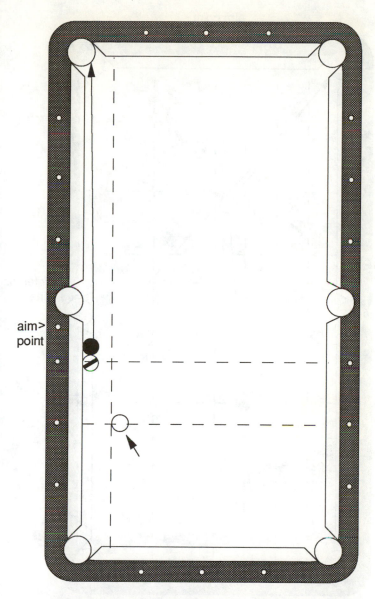

aim>
point

Beginners and Intermediates: The Combination Shot

Position the balls as shown. Align the cue stick through the center of
the ball and in line with the aim point. Parallel that line of aim in order
to strike the cue ball one and one half cue tips below the horizontal line
and one cue tip to the right of the vertical dividing line. Employ a firm
hard stroke using force eight. Object ball is 1/2 cut. Verified.

159

aim point
ⱽ

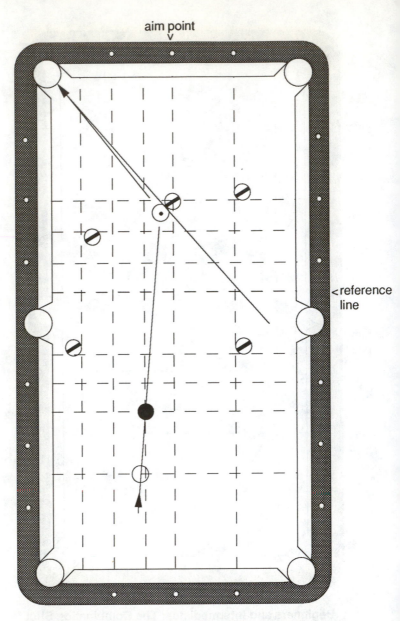

<reference
line

Beginners and Intermediate: The Kiss Shot

Place the balls in position as shown. To determine where and how the first object ball must strike the second object ball you need to know the location of the pocket in relation to the reference line. In this example you would strike the cue ball below the horizontal center and on the vertical axis line. Align the cue stick through the cue ball and in line with the aim point. Strike the cue ball with a firm soft stroke using force three. Hold the cue level. The first object ball will glance off the second object ball with a follow effect which will result in a well played shot. Verified.

160

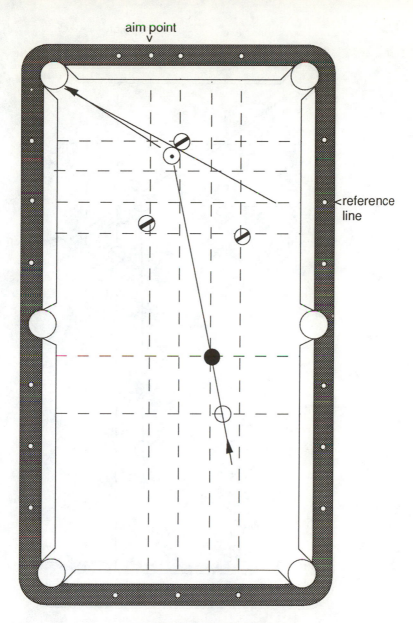

aim point

<reference line

Beginners and Intermediate: The Kiss Shot

Place the balls in position as shown. To determine where and how the first object ball must strike the second object ball you need to know the location of the pocket in relation to the reference line. In this example you would influence the object ball by striking the cue ball at the junction of the vertical and horizontal axis. Align the cue stick through the center of the cue ball and with the aim point. Strike the cue ball with a firm moderate stroke using force three. Rememeber to hold the cue level. Object ball is hit full. VERIFIED.

161

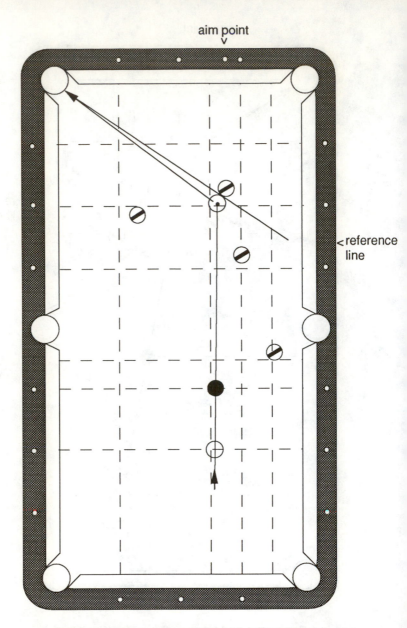

Beginners and Intermediates: The Kiss Shot

Place the balls in position as shown. To determine where and how the first object ball strikes the second object ball you need to know the location of the pocket in relation to the reference line. In this example you would strike the cue ball above the horizontal center and on the vertical axis line. Align the cue stick through the center of the cue ball and in line with the aim point. Employ a moderate stroke using force four. Hold the cue level. The first object ball will glance off the second object ball with a hold or draw effect resulting in a well played shot. Verified.

162

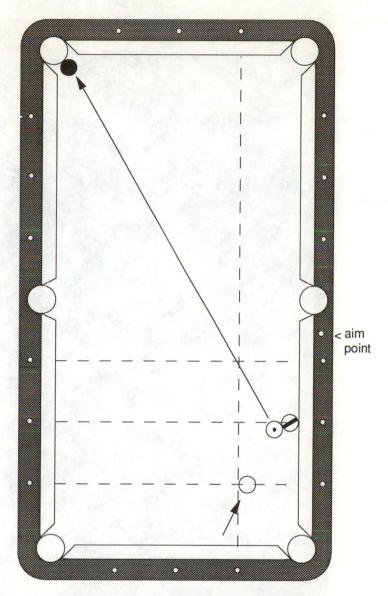

< aim
point

Beginners and Intermediates: The Kiss Shot

Place balls in position as shown. Align the cue stick through the center of the cue ball and in line with the aim point. Parallel that line of aim in order to strike the cue ball slightly above the horizontal line and slightly to the left of the vertical dividing line. Employ a firm soft stroke using force four. The first object ball needs to be "frozen" or touching the rubber cushion. Object ball is 1/2 cut. Verified.

Beg & Inter.-Kick -Cross Corner.-Raftis-O.H.

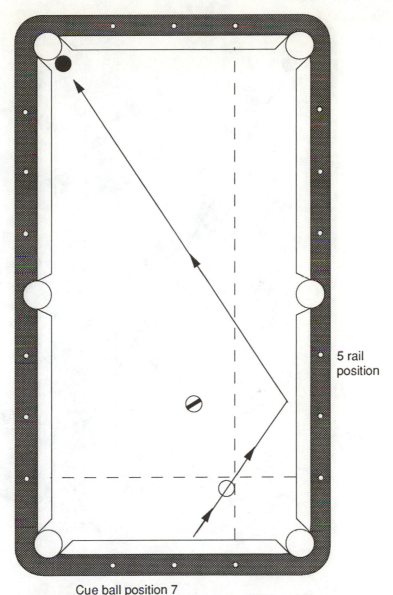

Cue ball position 7

Beginners and Intermediates: The draw shot

When the center of the cue ball is placed on the center of a line drawn from cue ball position seven to rail position five, then by striking the cue ball below the horizontal center and on the vertical dividing line, the cue ball will travel a path to pocket number four. Strike the cue ball with a firm soft stroke using force four. This shot pattern may be vey helpful for kick and bank shots. Verified . Photo.

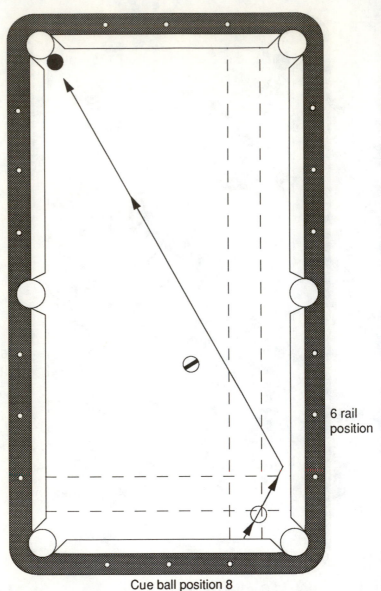

Cue ball position 8

Beginners and Intermediates: The draw shot

When the center of the cue ball is placed on the center of a line drawn from cue ball position eight to rail position six, then by striking the cue ball below the horizontal center and on the vertical dividing line, the cue ball will travel a path to pocket number four. Strike the cue ball with a firm soft stroke using force four. This shot pattern may be vey helpful for kick and bank shots. VERIFIED

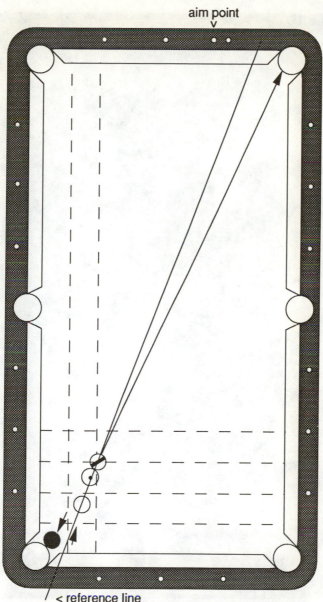

aim point
v

< reference line

Beginners and Intermediates: The Nip Draw

Place balls in position as shown. Align the cue stick through the center of the cue ball and in line with the aim point. Strike the cue ball below the horizontal center and on the vertical dividing line. Employ a quick sharp stroke using force five. The object is to drive the cue tip through the cue ball and onto the cloth. The cue must be quickly removed. Object ball is 3/4 cut. VERIFIED.

167

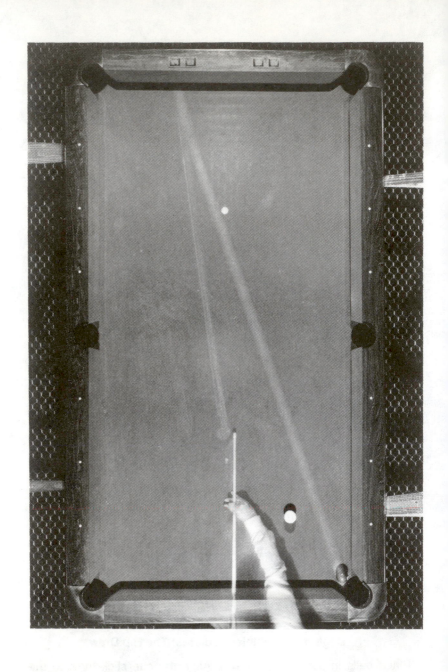

Beg. & Inter.-Draw Shot 114-C.Raftis-O.H.

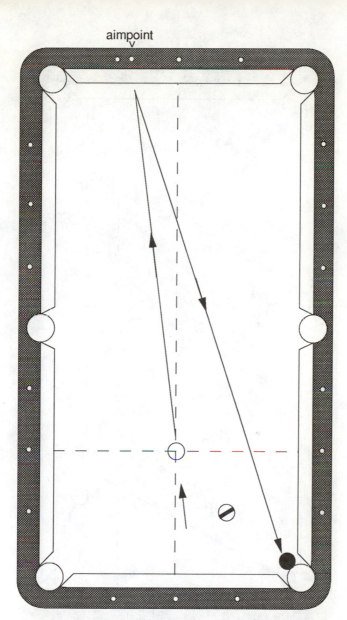

aimpoint

Beginners and Intermediates: The Draw Shot

Position balls as shown. Align cue stick through the center of the cue
ball and in line with the aim point. Parallel line of aim in order to strike
the cue ball below the horizontal center and to the right of the vertical
center. Strike the cue ball with a firm moderate stroke employing force
six. The object is to draw the cue ball off the rail as diagramed. This is
a stroke shot. Depending on the ability to stroke the cue ball properly
will depend on the degree of success obtainable on this shot. Object
ball is hit full. Verified. Photo.

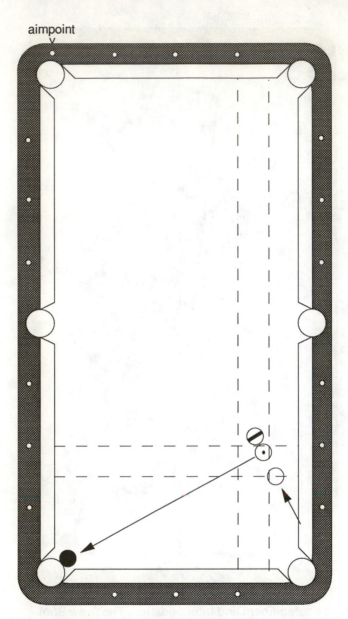

aimpoint

Beginners and Intermediates: The Draw Shot

Place the balls in position as shown. Align the cue stick through the center of the cue ball and in line with the aim point. Strike the cue ball one half of a cue tip below the horizontal dividing line. Employ a firm moderate stroke using force five. Object ball is 15/16 cut. VERIFIED.

aimpoint

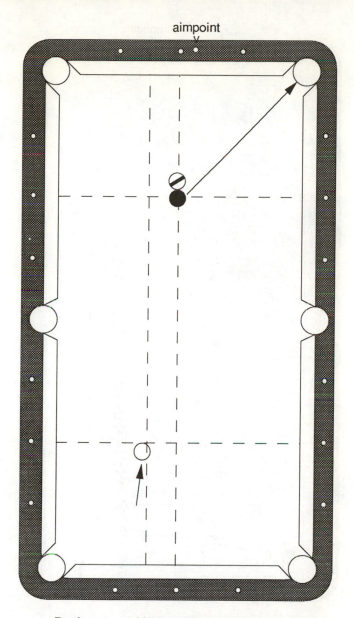

Beginners and Intermediates: The Draw Shot

Place the balls in position as shown. Align the cue stick through the center of the cue ball and in line with the aim point. Strike the cue ball two cue tips or six tenths of an inch below the horizontal center and on the vertical dividing line. Strike the cue ball with a firm moderate stroke using force six. Strike the first object ball straight on in the line of aim or full face just like a straight in shot. At first hold the cue level as practical then elevate the cue until you get the correct results. Object ball is hit full. VERIFIED.

171

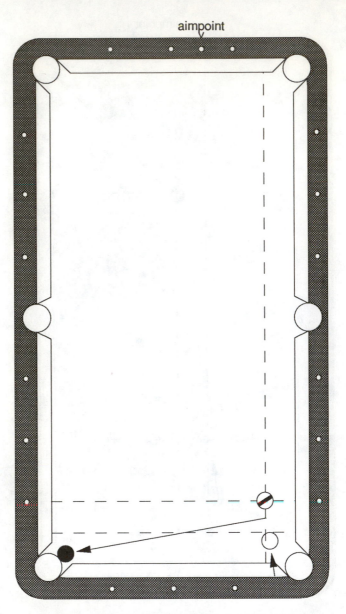

aimpoint

Beginners and Intermediates: The Draw Shot

Place balls in position as shown. Align cue stick through the center of
the cue ball and in line with the aim point. Strike the cue ball one cue
tip below the horizontal dividing line. Employ a firm moderate stroke
using force five. Object ball is 7/8 cut. Verified.

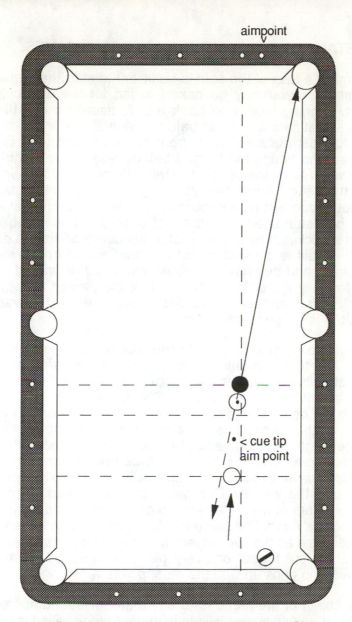

aimpoint

cue tip
aim point

Beginners and Intermediates: The Draw Shot

Place balls in position as shown. Make a club fist. Pretend that you want to hit something. Place your fist on the table in line with the shot pattern and with the palm touching the cloth. Place the cue stick between your thumb and index finger. Align the cue stick through the vertical center of the cue ball and below the horizontal center of the cue ball. Strike the cue ball with a moderate stroke using force four. Try to press the cue tip through the cue ball and onto the cloth at the reference shown. The cue ball should reverse after contact with the object ball. Object ball is 3/4 cut. Verified.

173

STARTING THE GAME AND DIFFERENT GAMES.

Normally a toss of the coin is sufficient to start the game. Sometimes you may be asked to lag for the option to start. Lagging means to bank a ball, usually a cue ball and sometimes an object ball, to the end rail or the rail the furthest distance away from the start, and then the player who brings the lagged ball closest to the starting rail would have the option to start. If you know that you are the better player then you may want to give the start to your opponent as a concession. The start of the game can be determined by a draw of a lower numbered ball from a pocket or by the draw of a numbered pill from a pill box. A pill is a small round ball that will fit in the ear chamber and that has a number imbedded or printed on it. Normally the order of play is that the person drawing the lowest number starts first, then the next lowest number is second and so forth.

One simple game to play is the oldest game known in pool and that is rotation or sixty-one. There are fifteen object balls available to play pool and in rotation or sixty-one all fifteen balls are used. When racking you will place the one ball in the apex position, the two and three balls at the corner positions and the fifteen ball in the center of the rack. The total numbers on the balls when added together total one hundred and twenty; therefore, the first player to pocket enough balls to total sixty-one is declared the winner. This game can be played by two, three or four players. When two or four players play then the play is normal because the four play as partners so it is the same as the two players playing. When three play it is called "cut throat" or every player for oneself. So the player who ends up with the most points wins.

The object of the game is to strike the lowest numbered ball first and whatever falls in is to your credit. So it is not the player who makes the most balls who wins; it is the player who pockets the balls with the highest numbers who wins. If you pocket an object ball and during the same shot pocket the cue ball then the object ball is placed on the foot spot and the cue ball is placed behind the head string. Then if the lower numbered ball is behind the head string it is placed on the foot spot and the pocketed ball is placed directly behind the lowest numbered ball.

Another game that is very popular for three-handed play or "cut throat" competition is to play "elimination". Elimination is played by the first shooter who strikes the rack selecting object balls one through five; the second shooter then selects the six through ten; and the last shooter the eleven through fifteen. The object is to pocket your opponent's balls before your opponent's pocket your balls. The player with a ball or balls left on the table is the winner. When a player's balls have all been pocketed then that player retires from the game and the other players continue.

I will discuss eight ball and nine ball games in separate chapters.

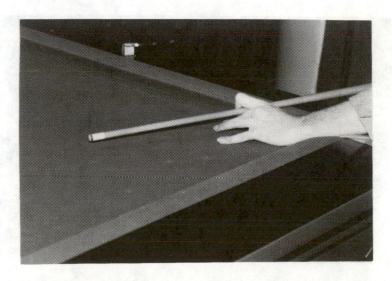

John Beyerlin on follow through   -angle view

Greg Dudzinski addressing cue ball-back view

Dominic Zito addressing cue ball   -side view

Dominic Zito addressing cue ball   -angle view

177

RACKING AND BREAKING.

When racking the balls the apex ball or the first ball in the rack is situated on the foot spot. The foot spot is an adhesive round dot attached to the cloth at the far end of the table or the end away from the break shot. If the balls are loosely racked (meaning that the balls do not touch one another in the rack) then they will not scatter when struck. The tighter the rack or the closer the balls are to touching then the better the break. One way to produce a tight rack is to situate the first ball in the rack exactly on the foot spot and then press the other balls forward so that they are touching. When you lift the rack (the rack is a wood or plastic form used to contain the balls) the balls should not move. If any movement is detected then you need to rerack the balls. Continue this process until you have a tight rack of balls. Another method that is not recommended is to impact the first three balls into the cloth by tapping them with a pool ball. This activity creates small impressions in the cloth and if done over a period of time by several players you may then find some holes or deep wear marks in the cloth.

Breaking the balls is an art. Some players seem to have a knack for the break shot. One thing that I have noticed about players who are able to make a few balls on the break occassionally is that they employ as much body movement as possible. I believe that an expert player can do away with all the body movement. A different process to follow is to extend the cue as far forward as possible with as quick a cue movement as possible. By accelerating the cue and maintaining ball contact you should be able to make a controlled break shot and pocket a few balls. I have made as many as four balls on an eight ball break using this method.

On the eight ball break I have found it practical to try to pocket the apex ball in the side pocket The idea is to place the cue ball to one side of the table behind the head string (the head string is an imaginary or drawn line

178

identifying the upper quarter of the table). Then by striking the cue ball above the horizontal center and slightly to the inside of the line from the cue ball to the apex ball and by striking the apex ball just off center at fifteen sixteenths and employing a hard stroke the apex ball should go towards the side pocket. With practice and determination you may be able to produce a series of these side pocket shots. Otherwise just strike the apex ball straight on with as much force as practical and hope for the best result. It could be advantageous to let your opponent break in eight ball especially if your opponent is the weaker player.

In nine ball the break is more important than in eight ball because in nine ball the game can be won on the break or by making a ball on the break the player may be able to run out the other balls. Trying to make the apex ball in the side pocket is one possibility. Another is to strike the apex ball straight on with as much force as possible. Yet another is to strike the apex ball straight on and at the same time to strike the cue ball below the horizontal center and to the right or left of the vertical center. By employing this procedure it is noticed that the corner ball in the rack sometimes goes straight into the corner pocket. It appears that the influence of english or spin on the break shot helps to pocket the corner ball in the rack. The secret of a good break is a strong follow through and the ability to move the cue rapidly through the cue ball. If you are using a jointed cue you may want to use a house cue or a straight cue for the break shot. There are two reasons for this; first, the end of the jointed cue may fracture or the cue tip may pop off; second, the one piece cue would appear to have a stronger spine and is able to bend upon impact with the cue ball and therefore add more force to the break shot.

Benjamin Jardin break shot   -front view

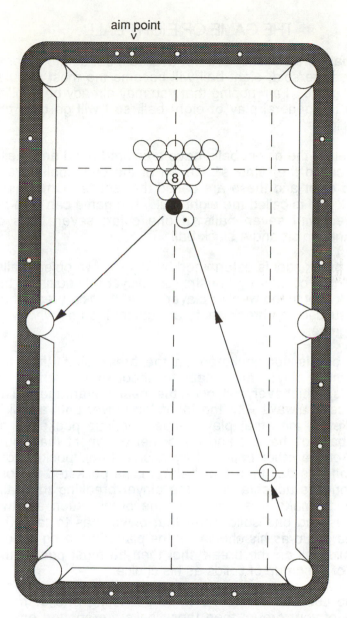

aim point

Beginners and Intermediates: The Break Shot

Place the balls as shown. Place aim point on rail. Align cue with aim point. Strike cue ball above center and slightly to the left or inside. Strike object ball off center to the right or outside, almost full. Use hard stroke using force eight. Object ball is 15/16 cut. VERIFIED

THE GAME OF EIGHT BALL .

Actually the statistics are not available but as more home tables are sold, eight ball will become the most popular pool game. I am hoping that you may already be familiar with the general play of eight ball, so I will go over the highlights.

Seven of the object balls have a colored band and these are called the "stripes". Seven of the other balls are a solid color and these are called the "solids". One ball is black and is called the eight ball. The game can also be played with seven balls of one color; seven balls of another color; and a black ball.

The break shot is determined by lagging two object balls; tossing a coin; or by the stronger player relinquishing the break shot to the weaker player. After the first break shot, the succeeding break shots are determined by who wins the game.

If a ball is not pocketed on the break shot, then the incoming player may elect to shoot at the stripes or solids; whichever will give the best advantage. The choice is always with the incoming player until a ball is pocketed, then that player must continue pocketing all the balls of that set and his or her opponent then must pocket the other balls. If by accident you pocket your opponent's ball then that ball remains pocketed to your opponent's advantage. If the player breaking the balls were to make three balls on the break; such as, two stripes and one solid, then that player has to take the stripe group as his choice. If the player breaking makes a solid ball on the break shot then he must pocket the rest of the group of solids as his choice.

If the cue ball scratches while pocketing one or more balls of your group, then those balls are spotted on the foot spot, one behind the other. If the cue ball scratches while pocketing one of your opponents balls or if one of your opponent's balls and one of your balls are pocketed, then your balls spot but the opponent's ball or balls stay pocketed.

The fifteen balls are racked with the apex ball on the foot spot and the eight ball is placed in the center of the rack; the other balls are mixed in the rack.

On the break shot it is difficult to make a ball consistently, but it is possible to make the apex ball or the front ball in the side pocket. Place the cue ball on one side of the table just below the head string and about one half of a diamond in from the long rail. Strike the cue ball above the horizontal center and just to the inside of the vertical center. Strike the object ball just off center-say fifteen sixteenths- with a hard strong stroke. The front ball should travel into the side pocket. With practice you may be able to make a few of these shots in succession.

Another method of breaking is to strike the front ball with as strong a force as possible and straight on.

If the eight ball is pocketed on the break, then it is spotted on the foot spot. If the eight ball is pocketed previous to the pocketing of the set of seven balls then the player pocketing the eight ball loses the game. If you pocket the eight ball and then scratch the cue ball then you lose the game. Another rule that some players use is when you are striking on the eight ball and you fail to hit the eight ball you lose the game.

When playing at eight ball there is no fixed consecutive order of shots; therefore, the opportunity for scoring is greater than in nine ball.

The object of the game of eight ball is to pocket the required eight balls before your opponent pockets his or her balls. If you are faced with a difficult shot in the sequence then you may want to play a safety. If your opponent has a ball in a pocket opening from which he can get easy position for the next shot and run out, then you may want to forfeit your turn at the table by pocketing the ball and leaving your opponent with a difficult shot.

If you are faced with a difficult shot then you will want to play safe or defensive. One method is to hide the cue ball behind an object ball. Another is to leave the cue ball as close to a rail as possible. Last is to knock your opponent's object ball away from a pocket opening.

When you read the table for a run out, you must select the principal ball or the seventh object ball so that you are able to secure good position on the eight ball. So the way you do this is to see where the position of the eight ball is and then try to find the seventh object ball. If when reading the table you are unable to locate the seventh object ball then you might want to consider playing a safety instead of going for a score.

In order to make a game with a weaker player, you might want to spot two object balls after the break shot. You need to always have the break shot when making this offer. When you select the two balls for your opponent, you will want to consider if the selected balls are to be used offensively or defensively. In other words you take two balls that will clear your seven balls or you take two balls that your opponent would have scored anyway. One other alternative is to leave your opponent safe by removing two balls that are in easy striking distance or by not removing balls that are near your opponent's cue ball, so as to leave your opponent a difficult scoring position. Sometimes it is easier to win by giving your opponent a spot of two balls because automatically, the nature of the game is changed and you exercise more control over the results.

Some rule variations are as follows: To pocket the eight ball in the same pocket as the seventh ball; this variation is called "last pocket". To pocket the one ball in the side pocket and the fifteen ball in the other side pocket, according to your group, before pocketing the eight ball. To play to bank the eight ball on a called shot. The rules may vary from district to district, so check first before playing.

It is also possible to play a shorter rack of eight ball by playing with nine balls; four stripes; four solids; and the eight ball. The balls are racked in a diamond shape. The eight ball is placed in the middle and the other balls are mixed in the rack. The object of the game is the same as outlined previously. Three advantages can be seen: the first is that it is easier to make the break shot; second, there is less chance of clusters; and third, the game plays in one half the time required for the fifteen ball game.

Dominic Zito on follow through   -front view

THE NINE BALL GAME.

In the game of nine ball it is very important to develop a good break shot. In order to execute a good break shot, the cue stick should accelerate rapidly with a good follow through. In order to have a good impact and large ball movement it is necessary that the apex ball be struck full face. A well hit cue ball should travel at approximately twenty five miles per hour for a male adult player and twenty miles an hour for an adult female player. This fact was reported by another author who measured the distance and took the time from the frames of a camcorder.

One object on the break shot could be to pocket the apex ball in the side pocket. This is done by striking the cue ball above the horizontal dividing line and striking the object ball slightly off center to the outside; or approximately a fifteen sixteenths hit on the object ball. It may help to strike the cue ball slightly off center to the inside of the hit, say one half of a cue tip to the inside. If executed successfully the apex ball will rebound from the rack into the side pocket. One thing that I forgot to mention was where to place the cue ball for the break shot. Place the cue ball just below the head string and approximately one half of a diamond's distance from the long rail. This is not a sure thing, but with a little practice you will make some of these shots and the occasional ball pocketed will help your game.

The game of nine ball is played by racking nine balls numbered consecutively from one through nine into a diamond shape with the one ball as the apex ball and the nine ball or striped ball placed in the center of the racked balls. The tighter the rack the better the distribution of balls on the break. After the break shot the object balls are struck in consecutive order, the lowest number first, until the nine ball is pocketed, which ends the game.

One variation of play is that the five ball becomes a second winning object ball and it is then placed at the end of the pyramid rack.

186

Another variation of play is that the nine ball must be pocketed as the last ball to complete the game; therefore, each time the nine ball is pocketed previous to the last ball it is a win.

One condition of play in nine ball is that when a foul is committed, the cue ball is in hand, meaning that you are allowed to pick up the cue ball and place it wherever it suits your best interests. A foul means to pocket the cue ball, move a ball accidentally and return it to it's former position without your opponent's consen,; to not strike a rail after contacting an object ball, or to jump the cue ball off the table.

The one exception to this rule is on the break shot. If a foul is committed on the break shot then the cue ball is in hand behind the head string.

Many players like to play "all down stay down", which means that if you have the cue ball in hand after the break shot and your desired object ball is behind the head string, then you are allowed to pocket the desired ball by hand. Also if the cue ball enters a pocket after an object ball is pocketed, then the object ball remains pocketed unless it is the nine ball. The same rule is true if the cue ball jumps the table after pocketing an object ball. If an object ball is pocketed accidentally by hand then that ball also would remain pocketed unless it was the nine ball. If the nine ball has to be placed on the table after illegal pocketing then it should be replaced at the approximate position it occupied previous to the accident or be placed on the foot spot, to be determined by the opposing player.

Sometimes a push is allowed. An example of a push is as follows: when there are obstructing balls between the cue ball and the desired object ball then yiou may take the side of the cue near the tip and strike the cue ball so that the cue ball is in the open or so that the path between the cue ball and the desired object ball is clear. The incoming player then has a choice; either to shoot or allow you to shoot again. A push may be allowed on the

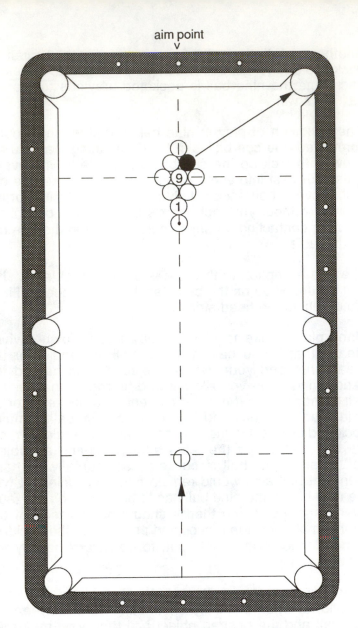

aim point
v

Beginners and Intermediates: The Break Shot

Place the balls in position as shown. Align the cue stick through the center of the cue ball and in line with the aim point. Parallel that line of aim in order to strike the cue ball below the horizontal dividing line and to the left of the vertical dividing line. Employ full force and a hard stroke. Women use force eight and men force ten. The one ball or apex ball is struck full. If the english is applied to the other side then the opposite ball would go in the corner. Object ball is hit full. VERIFIED.

shot following the break shor or when a scratch means an additional penalty.

If you cannot make all the balls in consecutive order, then it may become necessary to play a safety. There are several ways to play a safety. First there is a snooker. A snooker means that the cue ball or desired object ball is behind another ball or group of balls; in other words one of the balls is hidden so that direct contact is not possible. To get out of a snooker it is necessary to play one of the following shots: a kick; a jump or a curve.

Another thing that you can do if you feel that you cannot make all the balls in order is to play a lag. By striking the object ball thin and with a soft force, you can lag the cue ball to the farthest rail or to a nearby rail, hoping for a freeze on the rail. The shot then becomes more difficult because you can only strike the cue ball above center with an elevated cue and the distance between the cue ball and the desired object ball helps to make the shot more difficult.

Other things to do are to strike the object ball so that it travels to a rail hoping for a freeze. Next is to strike the object ball so that when it stops your opponent will be left with a difficult shot.

When playing at nine ball it is always necessary to plan ahead as many shots as is practical. Every player does not read the table the same; therefore, what is correct for one player may not be correct for another player. Although in many situations a similar pattern will develop.

One method of playing position is to leave the cue ball near the object ball and the shortest distance from the previous object ball. Another method is to play the speed of the cue ball for position on the second object ball. In other words you make a normal cut shot but by utilizing more or less force on the cue ball you plan to arrive at a favored position for the next shot. One method is to always play to score the sure shots and to play safe on a difficult shot.

The idea of strategy is to visualize how you can score your shots and at the same time make it difficult for your opponent to score his shots.

A definition of a legal shot is that you struck a desired object ball after which the desired object ball, another ball or the cue ball contacted a rail or you pocketed an object ball. The exception to this rule is when the object ball is frozen (touching the cushion), then it becomes necessary to contact another cushion with the cue ball or object ball.

Many nine ball matches are played as a run to seven. Instead of seven it could be any number. A run to a number means that when a player wins the specified number of games, then he wins the match. Sometimes this activity is know as a "freeze out".

When playing a freeze out, the player who is able to gain the lead could be called a front runner. A front runner may be able to take more risks than the player who is behind. An example would be that a front runner when faced with a difficult shot pattern that would normally require playing a safety would shoot out for a score instead, hoping to increase the win total and the match.

Many players will tell you that your best defense is a good offense.

Along these same lines some tournament conductors and players like to use the rule that three consecutive fouls during a game becomes a loss of the game. After the offending player has committed two fouls, the opponent must warn him of the foul trouble before the opportunity to commit the third foul; otherwise, the foul count remains at two.

One strategy when playing against a front runner is to try to increase the amount of safeties that you play so as to wear him down and not give him an opportunity to run out. The same strategy can be applied towards a player who enjoys shooting out. A shoot out player tries to score all the shots in succession and doesn't attempt a safety play. This style of player is most difficult to defeat. When he is "on his game" you might say that he is impossible to defeat.

When "reading the table" it is good to know what your shot percentages are in order to determine if you will go all out for the shot; play for easy position; play for hard position; play a half safety; or play a full safety. Your judgement should be based on how well you are able to score the shot in front of you. One consideration when reading the table is at what point does the percentage shot appear in the game. If a low percentage shot appears as the final shot in the game, then you may want to go for it. If the same shot appears early in the game you would probably play a safety.

Another example would be that if you have been practicing difficult cut shots into the corner pocket using a mechanical bridge and you have scored six out of nine shots then your chances of scoring would be two to one in your favor. So if the game is a close match you might not want to take the chance of the miss. Of course, if you are in front in the match then the risk might not be as great; also if your opponent is a much weaker player then the risk also would not be as great.

Many times you will need to plan several shots ahead. In this way you will be able to plan how to break out clusters from the rail to improve your shot making opportunities.

The more knowledge you have about bank angles and cut shots the easier it is to play out of trouble; such as making a kick shot when you are snookered.

On occasion it may be advisable to pocket a ball out of sequence; such as, when the nine ball is in or near a pocket and you don't have a good scoring opportunity.

The game is started by each player lagging an object ball to the starting rail and the closest ball winning the lag. Another method of starting is to flip a coin. And yet another is to relinquish the break shot to the weaker player.

When you become a strong nine ball player you may have to spot a ball or balls to make a game. First you would spot the eight ball; which means that any time during the game that your opponent pockets the eight or nine he wins the game. If you have difficulty making a game spotting the eight ball then you can add a seven ball spot. If there is still difficulty then you have to give the break shot option. This is the limit. If you still cannot make a match then you have to give a game concession; such as, I'll play to seven games while you play to three games.

Benjamin Jardin's back swing   -side view

Benjamin Jardin prior to stroke   -front view

Benjamin Jardin on follow through-side view

PRACTICE SHOTS: ADVANCED AND EXPERT.

The following shots are illustrated according to the degree of skill needed to perfect the shot. All of the shots illustrated are drawn to scale for a four foot by eight foot pool table, this being the most common size table in use today. The shot patterns are verified, either by an exposed overhead camera shot or by a participant actually playing and making the shot. A few shots that are illustrated depend on The skill level of the individual player and Those special shots have been so identified.

For bar lounge players, all the shots have been tested on a Valley Recreation table three and one half feet wide and seven feet long.

I wish you every success in making these shots. When you finish this section, you may want to try the fancy shots in the next section for use in performing exhibitions or just to impress your friends and associates.

A final note: If you practice the same shot over and over, you may want to use a removable, self-adhesive ring binder reinforcement for locating the ball.

Dominic Zito rail bridge   -angle view

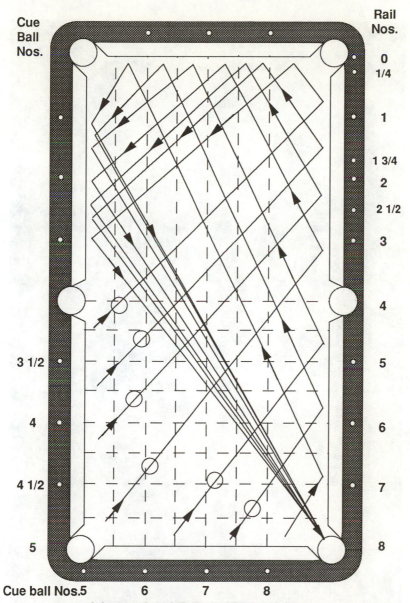

0
1/4

1

1 3/4
2

2 1/2

3

4

3 1/2   5

4   6

4 1/2   7

5   8

Cue ball Nos.5   6   7   8

Advanced and Expert - diamond system

The diagram represents the ball tracks for playing bank or kick shots into the corner pocket. It is necessary to strike the cue ball at the junction of the vertical and horizontal centers. Employ a firm moderate stroke using force five and one half. As the entry angle into the side rail increases you similarly need to strike the cue ball slightly below center in order to make a strong rail contact and eliminate the possibility of slide. When the cue ball is near a corner then that corner becomes cue ball position five and the rail numbers start from the far corners at zero. The aim point may vary according to the playability of the rubber cushions. Verified.

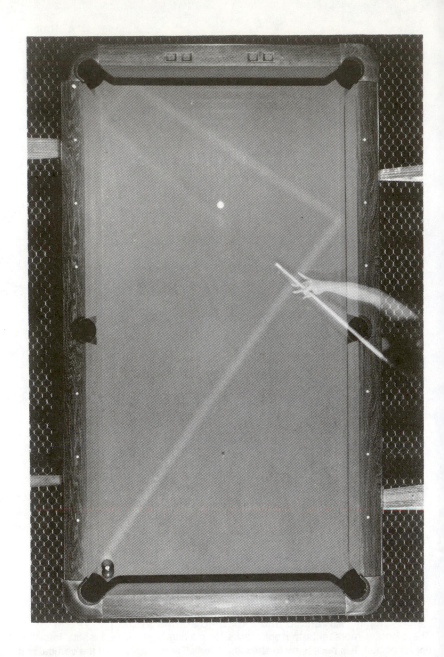

Adv. and Expert-Diamond Sys. 149-K.Ann-O.H.

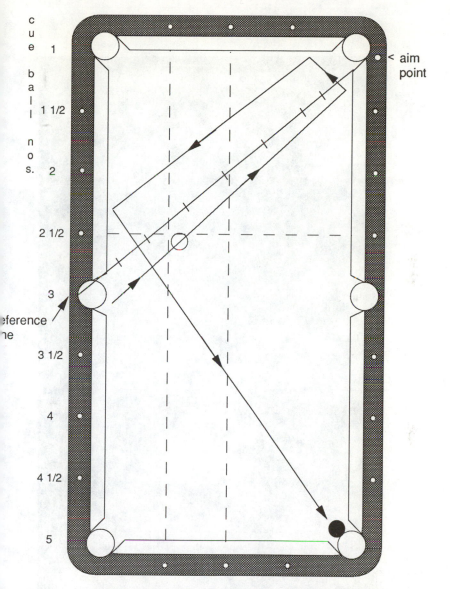

Advanced and Expert: The Diamond System

A reference line is drawn from cue ball position three to rail position zero. The actual ball track will run parallel from cue ball position number three and one quarter to position one quarter. The destination of the cue ball is pocket number one. Strike the cue ball at the junction of the vertical and horizontal axis. Use force number four or a moderate force. If you have trouble with this shot then strike the cue ball one quarter of an inch to the left of the vertical center line or one half of a cue tip from the center line to the left. Object ball is hit full. Verified. Photo.

197

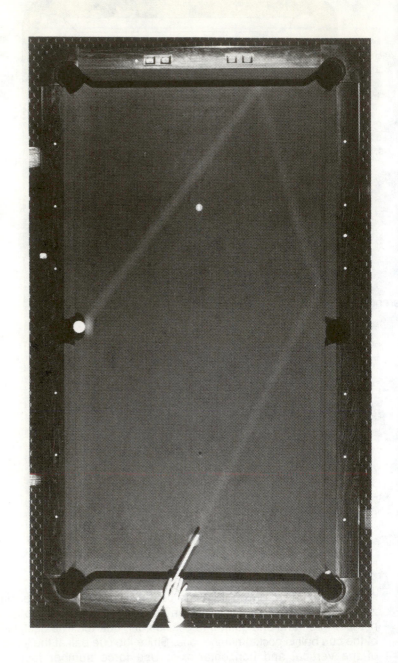

Adv and Expert-Kick Shot 2 rails -Raftis-O.H.

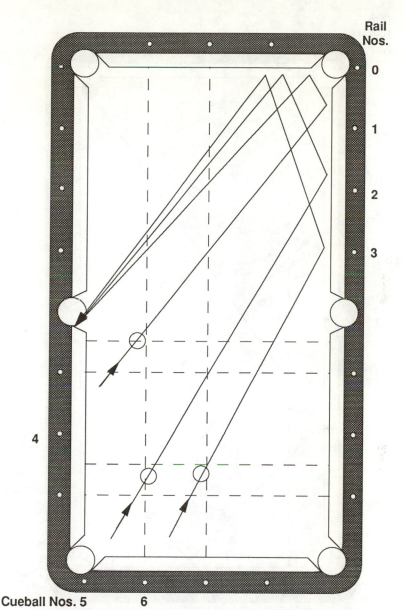

Cueball Nos. 5   6

Advanced and Expert: diamond system - 2 rails long in the side

The diagram represents the ball tracks for playing kick or bank shots for the side pocket. It is necessary to strike the cue ball at hte junction of the vertical and horizontal division lines. Hold the cue level. Strike the cue ball with a firm moderate stroke using force three and one half. Other ball tracks can be produced by paralleling or interpretation. The objective is pocket number three. The system is that by knowing the cue ball position number and knowing the destination rail number then you only need to subtract to find the aim point number. It may be necessary to add one half cue tip of english on the left of the cue ball. Verified see Photo

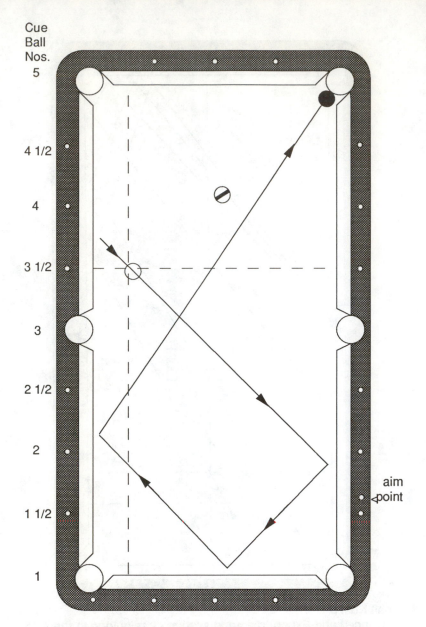

Cue Ball Nos.

5

4 1/2

4

3 1/2

3

2 1/2

2

1 1/2

1

aim point

Advanced and Expert: Diamond System

The cue ball is located on cue ball position number four. Strike the cue ball in the direction on aim point at rail position one and one quarter. Use force number four. Strike the cue ball at the conjunction of the vertical and horizontal centers. The objective is pocket number four. Remember that the center line of the cue stick passes over the center of the rail marker. VERIFIED.

200

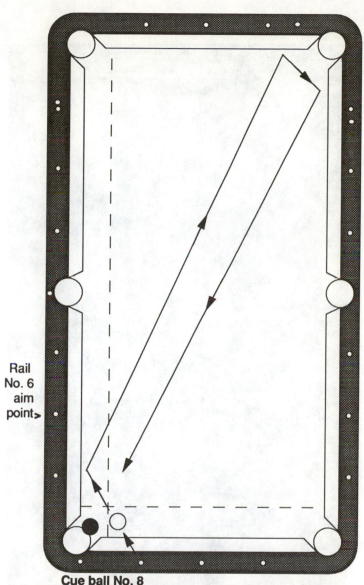

Rail
No. 6
aim
point>

Cue ball No. 8
Advanced and Expert: Diamond System

The cue ball is located on cue ball position number 8. Place the center of the cue ball on the line drawn from C.B. 8 to rail position 6. Align the cue stick through the center of the cue ball and in line with the aim point. Strike the cue ball on the vertical dividing line and slightly below the horizontal dividing line. Strike the cue ball with a moderate stroke using force five. Things to remember: The center of the cue travels over the center of the rail marker. VERIFIED.

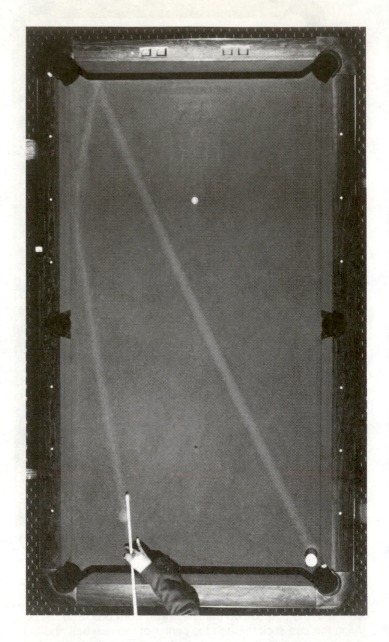

Advanced and Expert 2 rail kick #2 C.Raftis

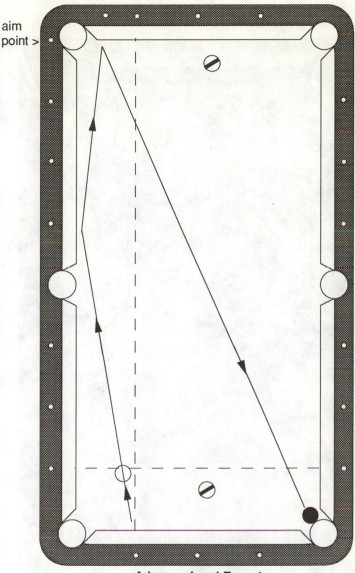

aim
point >

**Advanced and Expert
diamond system**

The cue ball is located on cue ball position number eight. The center of
the cue ball should be on the ball track line shown on the diagram. Strike
the cue ball below the horizontal center of the cue ball and favoring the
right of the vertical axis line. Use force number five or a moderate force
that will take the cue ball past the objective, which is pocket number one.
On this shot the important consideration is to avoid a slide off the rail after
contact so elevate the cue 22 1/2°. VERIFIED PHOTO

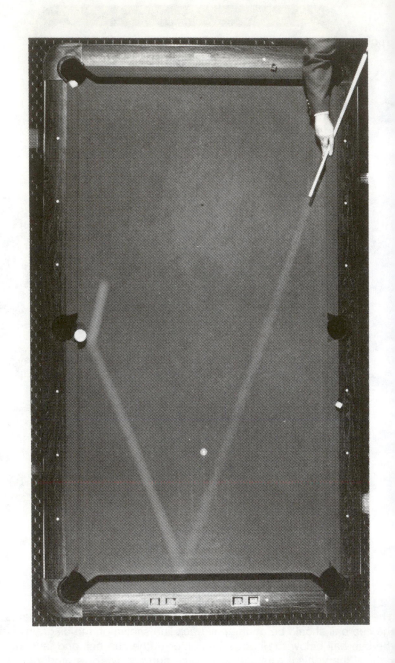

Adv.and Expert-Kick Shot-1 rail -Raftis-O.H.

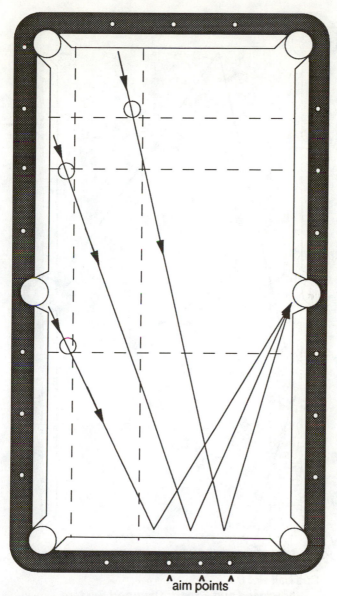

^aim ^points^

Advanced and Expert - The Kick Shot: one rail long into the side

The diagram represents the ball tracks for kicking or banking a ball into the side pocket. Other ball tracks can be created by interpretation. Strike the cue ball in the center at the junction of the vertical and horizontal dividing lines. Employ a firm soft stroke using force four. One objective is to avoid striking the near corner of the side pocket. Hold the cue level and do not change your posture until after the ball has contacted the rubber cushion. **VERIFIED PHOTO**

205

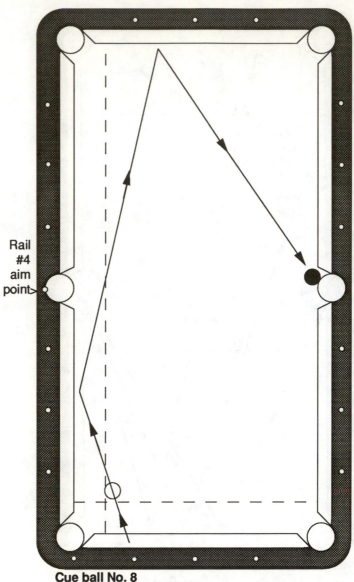

Rail
#4
aim
point

Cue ball No. 8
Advanced and Expert: Diamond System

The cue ball is located on cue ball position number eight Strike cue ball below center in direction of aim point. the cue ball will rebound with imparted influence to pocket number 6. Use force number four in order to grab the rail and to keep the cue ball from sliding. Center line of cue ball and cue stick must be in relationship to drawn line. VERIFIED.

aim point

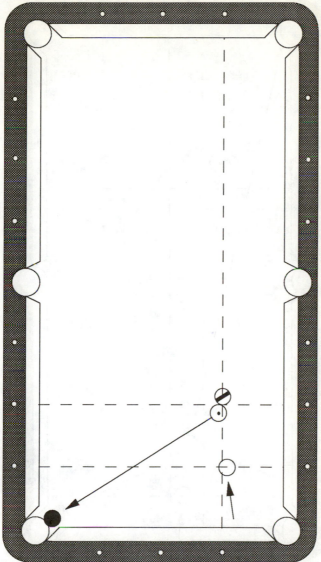

Advanced and Expert: The Draw Shot

Place the balls in position as shown. Align the cue stick through the center of the cue ball and in line with the aim point. Strike the cue ball one and one half cue tips below the horizontal dividing line. Employ a moderate stroke employing force six. Remember to allow the cue tip to follow through the cue ball to the cloth. Object ball is 3/4 cut. VERIFIED.

aim point

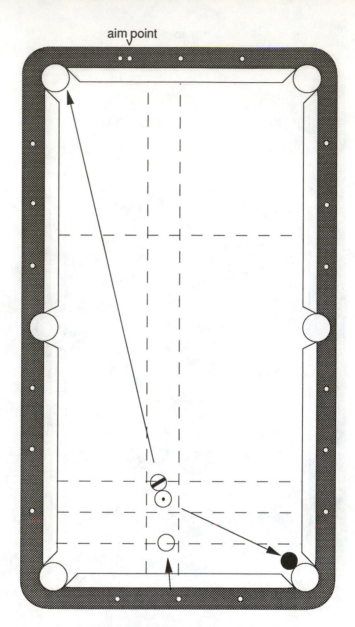

Advanced and Expert: The Draw Shot

Place the balls in position as shown. Align the cue stick through the
center of the cue ball and in line with the aim point. Strike the cue ball
one and one half cue tips below the horizontal center and on the
vertical dividing line. Strike the cue ball with a firm soft stroke using
force three. Remember to follow through with the cue tip to the cloth.
Object ball is 7/8 cut. Verified.

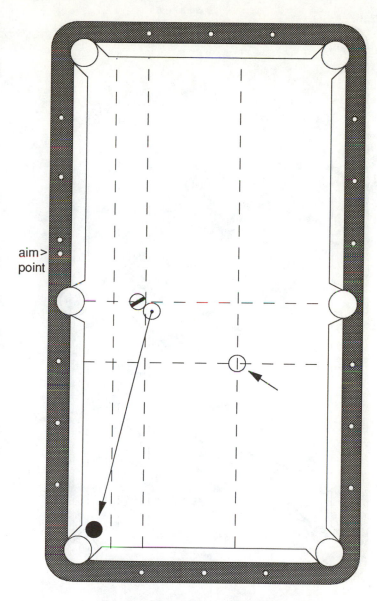

aim >
point

Advanced and Expert: The Draw Shot

Place the balls in position as shown. Align the cue stick through the center of the cue ball and in line with the aim point. Parallel that line of aim in order to strike the cue ball one and one half cue tips below the horizontal dividing line and one cue tip to the left of the vertical dividing line. Employ a firm moderate stroke using force five. Remember to allow the cue tip to follow through to the cloth. Object ball is 3/4 cut. VERIFIED.

209

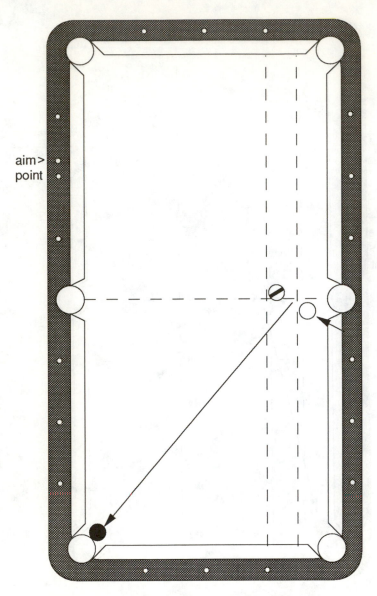

aim>
point

Advanced and Expert: The Draw Shot

Place the balls in position as shown. Align the cue stick through the center of the cue ball and in line with the aim point. Strike the cue ball one cue tip below the horizontal dividing line and on the vertical dividing line. Employ a firm moderate stroke using force five. The balls are close together so employ a short follow through with a quick wrist movement. Object ball is 3/4 cut. VERIFIED.

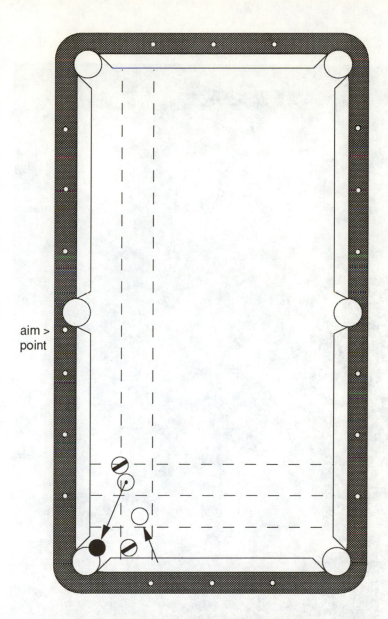

aim >
point

Advanced and Expert: The Draw Shot

Place the balls in position as shown. Align the cue stick through the center of the cue ball and in line with the aim point. Strike the cue ball one cue tip below the horizontal line and on the vertical dividing line. Employ a firm soft stroke using force three. Here the action is quick so employ a short follow through with a quick wrist movement. Object ball is 15/16 cut. Verified

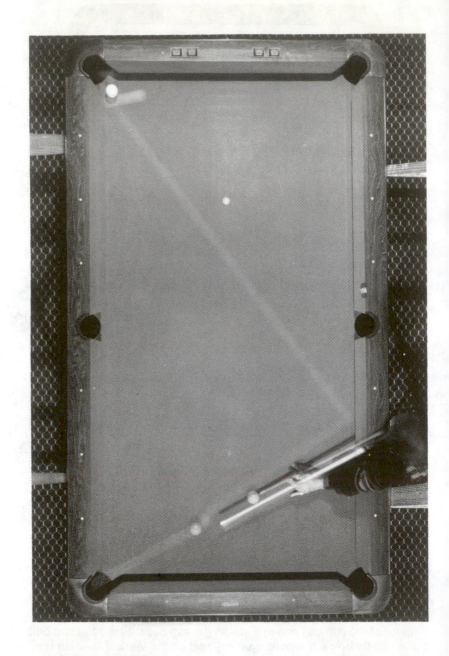

Adv. and Expert-Draw Shot 78-B.Carson-O.H.

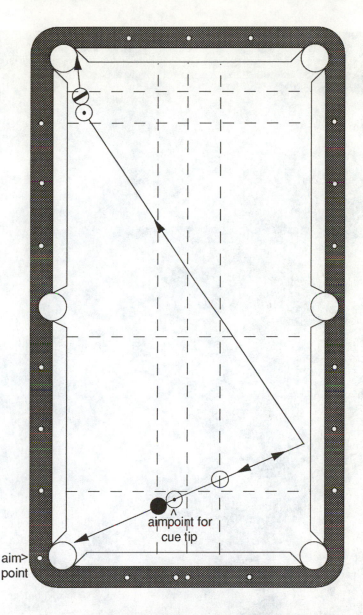

aim>
point

aimpoint for
cue tip

Advanced and Expert: The Draw Shot

Place the balls in position as shown. Align the cue stick through the center of the cue ball and in line with the aim point. Strike the cue ball below the horizontal center and one half cue tip or one quarter inch to the left of the vertical center. Use a moderate strong stroke employing force force six. Press the cue stick through the cue ball and into the cloth at the recommended aim point shown on the schematic. This will ensure the long draw action. The cue ball will assume an english or spin influence after contacting the rubber cushion and the cue ball will travel in the direction indicated. Object ball is hit full. Shot depends on skill level. Verified with photo.

213

Adv..and Expert-Draw Shot 77-B.Carson-O.H.

214

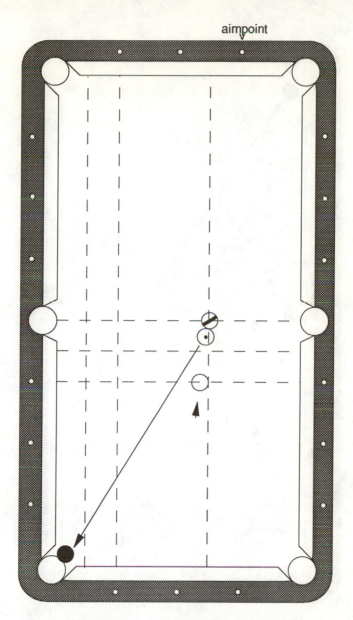

aimpoint

Advanced and Expert: The Draw Shot

Place the balls in position as shown. Align the cue stick through the
center of the cue ball and in line with the aim point. Strike the cue ball
one and one half cue tips below the horizontal dividing line. Employ a
firm moderate stroke and use force six. Remember to allow the cue tip
to follow through to the cloth. Object ball is 15/16 cut. Verified depends
on skill level. Photo.

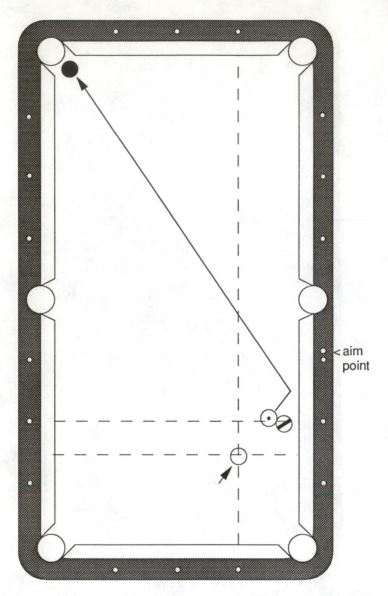

Advanced and Expert: The Draw Curve

Position balls as shown. Align the cue stick through the center of the
cue ball and in line with the aim point. Parallel that line of aim in order
to strike the cue ball one and one half cue tips below the horizontal line
and one and one half cue tips to the right of the vertical dividing line.
Employ a firm hard stroke using force eight. Object ball is 1/32 cut.
Verified.

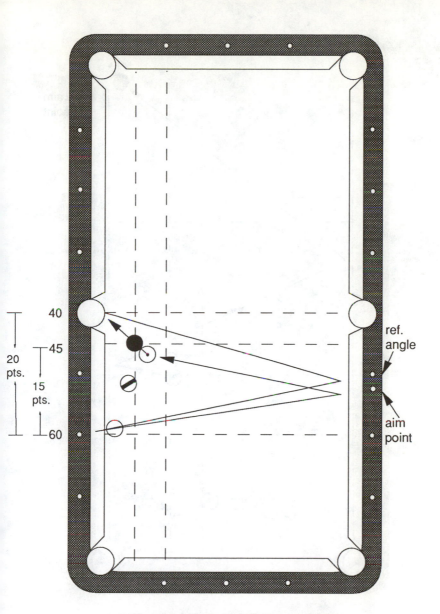

Advanced and Expert: The Kick Shot

Place balls in position as shown. Align cue stick through the center of the cue ball and in line with the aim point. Strike the cue ball on the vertical center line. Employ a firm soft stroke using force three. What has been done here is that half of the difference between the reference angle and the object ball position has been subtracted on the rail to arrive at a new aim point. In other words one quarter of a diamond has been subtracted. Object ball is 1/2 cut.

217

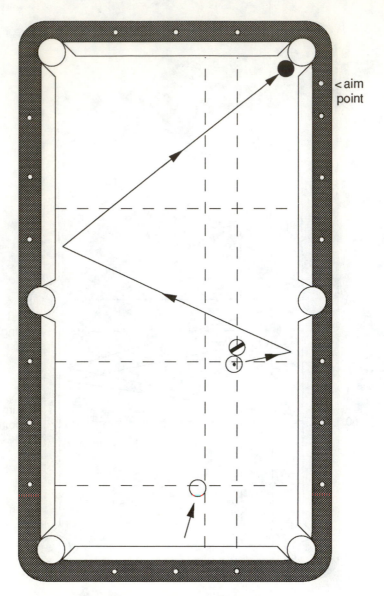

< aim point

Advanced and Expert: The Kick Shot

Place the balls in position as shown. Align the cue stick through the center of the cue ball and in line with the aim point. Parallel that line of aim in order to strike the cue ball one cue tip below the horizontal line and slightly to the left of the vertical dividing line. Employ a firm moderate stroke using force five and one half. Object ball is 5/8 cut. Verified.

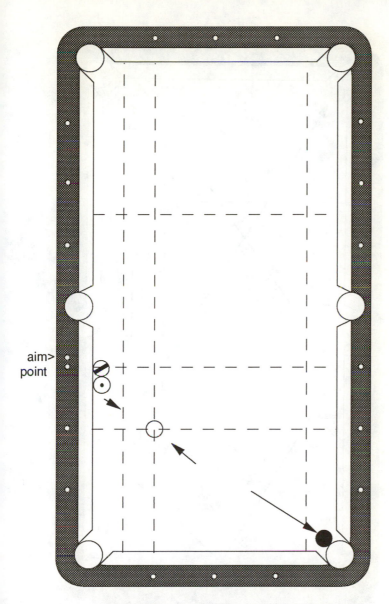

aim>
point

Advanced and Expert: The Kick Shot

Place the balls in position as shown. Align the cue stick through the center of the cue ball and in line with the aim point. Parallel that line of aim in order to strike the cue ball one cue tip below the horizontal line and one cue tip to the left of the vertical dividing line. Employ a firm moderate stroke using force five. Object ball is 1/8 cut. VERIFIED.

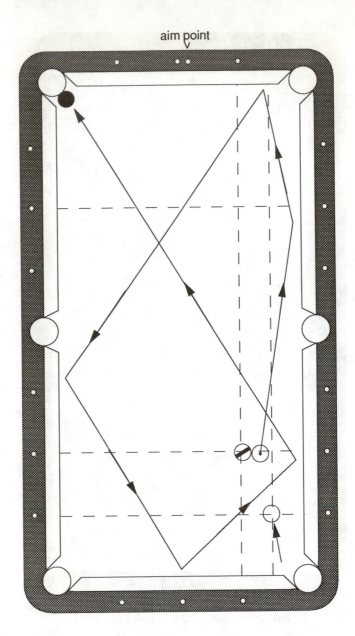

aim point

Advanced and Expert: The Kick Shot

Place the balls in position as shown. Align the cue stick through the center of the cue ball and in line with the aim point. Parallel the line of aim in order to strike the cue ball slightly below center and one cue tip to the left of the vertical center. Strike the cue ball with a firm hard stroke using force nine. Object ball is 1/16 cut. Verified.

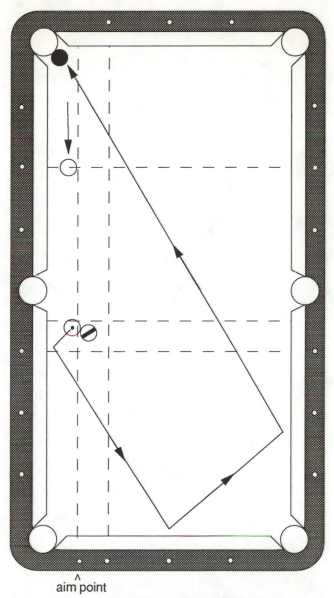

aim point

Advanced and Expert: The Kick Shot

Place the balls in position as shown. Align the cue stick through the center of the cue ball and in line with the aim point. Parallel the line of aim in order to strike the cue ball one half of a cue tip below the horizontal center and one cue tip to the left of the vertical center. Strike the cue ball with a firm moderate stroke using force six. Object ball is 1/3 cut. Verified.

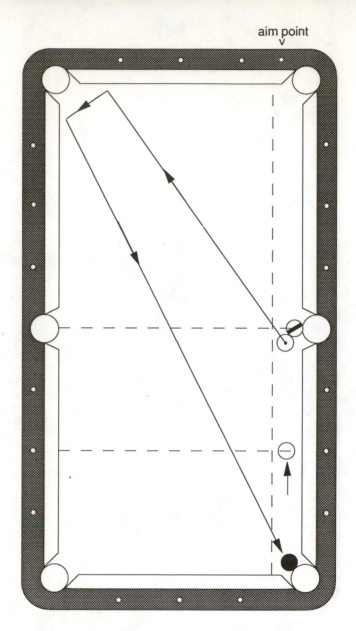

aim point

Advanced and Expert: The Kick Shot

Place the balls in position as shown. Align the cue stick through the center of the cue ball and in line with the aim point. Parallel that line of aim in order to strike the cue ball one half of a cue tip above the horizontal line and very slightly to the left of the vertical center line. Strike the cue ball with a firm soft stroke using force four. Object ball is 5/8 cut. Verified.

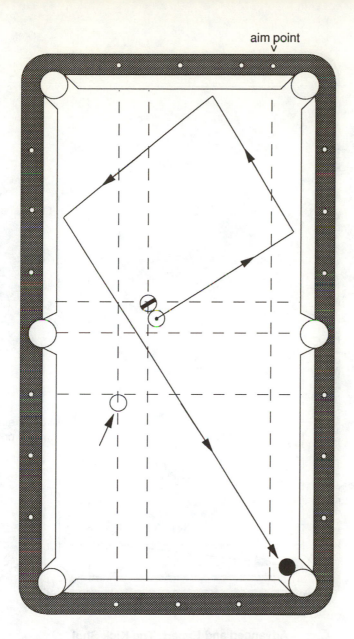

aim point

Advanced and Expert: The Kick Shot

Place the balls in position as shown. Align the cue stick through the center of the cue ball and in line with the aim point. Parallel that line of aim in order to strike the cue ball at the horizontal dividing line and one and one half cue tips to the left of the vertical dividing line. Strike the cue ball with a firm moderate stroke using force six. Object ball is 1/4 cut. Verified.

223

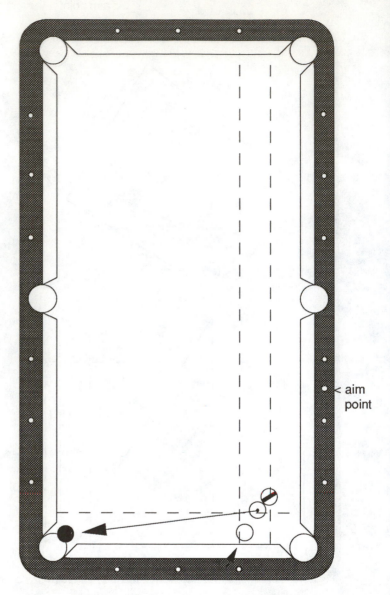

aim
point

Advanced and Expert: The Kick Shot

Place the balls in position as shown. Align the cue stick through the center of the cue ball and in line with the aim point. Parallel that line of aim in order to strike the cue ball slightly below the horizontal dividing line and slightly to the right of the vertical dividing line. Employ a firm moderate stroke using force five. Object ball is 15/16 cut.

aimpoint
v

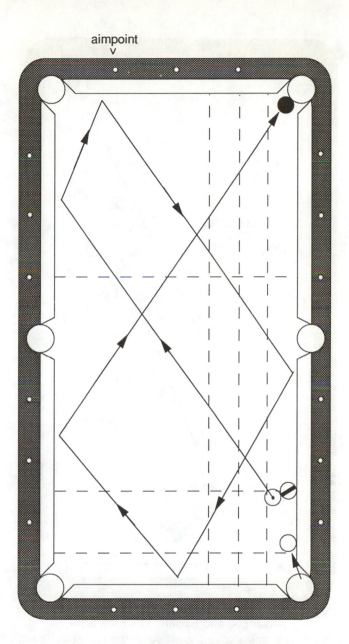

Advanced and Expert: The Kick Shot

Place the balls in position as shown. Align the cue stick through the center of the cue ball and in line with the aim point. Parallel that line of aim in order to strike the cue ball slightly below the horizontal dividing line and one and one half cue tips to the right of the vertical dividing line. Strike the cue ball hard using force nine. Object ball is 1/8 cut. Verified.

225

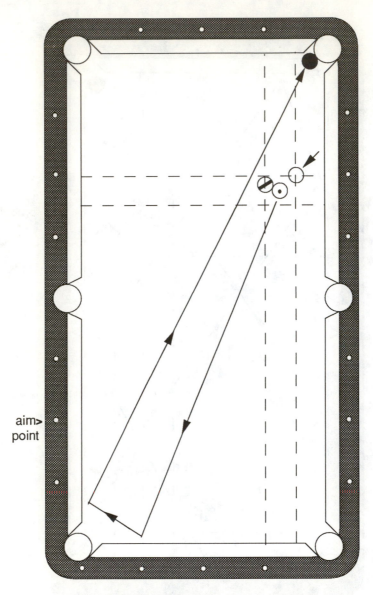

aim>
point

Advanced and Expert: The Kick Shot

Place the balls in position as shown. Align the cue stick through the center of the cue ball and in line with the aim point. Parallel that line of aim in order to strike the cue ball one half of a cue tip to the right of the vertical center. Employ a soft stroke using force four. Verified.

226

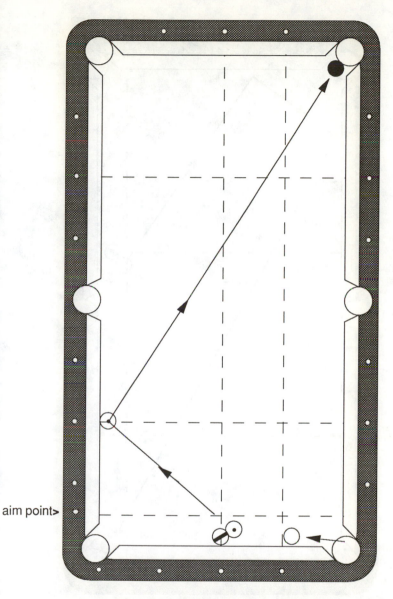

aim point>

Advanced and Expert: The Kick Shot

Place balls in position as shown. Align the cue stick through the
center of the cue ball and in line with the aim point. Paralell that line
of aim in order to strike the cue ball one half a cue tip to the right of
the vertical center. Strike the cue ball with a firm soft stroke using
force four. VERIFIED.

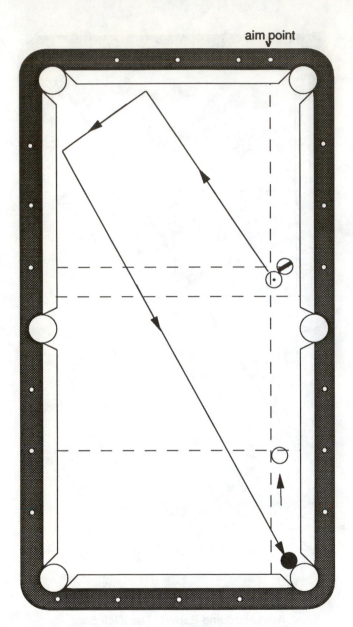

Advanced and Expert: The Kick Shot

Place the balls in position as shown. Align the cue stick through the center of the cue ball and in line with the aim point. Paralell the line of aim in order to strike the cue ball one half of a cue tip above the horizontal line and slightly left of the vertical dividing line. Strike the cue ball with a firm soft stroke using force four. **VERIFIED**

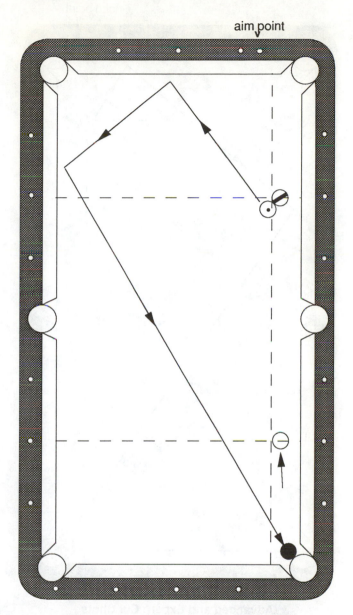

aim point

Advanced and Expert: The Kick Shot

Place the balls in position as shown. Align the cue stick through the center of the cue ball and in line with the aim point. Paralell the line of aim in order to strike the cue ball one half of a cue tip above the horizontal line and slightly left of the vertical dividing line. Strike the cue ball with a firm soft stroke using force four. Object ball is 1/4 cut. Angle cue 10°. Verified.

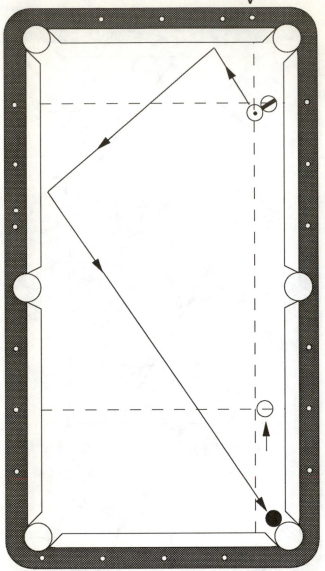

aim point

Advanced and Expert: Cut Shots

Place balls in position as shown. Align the cue stick through the center of the cue ball and in line with the aim point. Paralell the line of aim in order to strike the cue ball one half of a cue tip above the center and one cue tip to the left of the vertical dividing line. Strike the cue ball with a firm moderate stroke using force six. Verified.

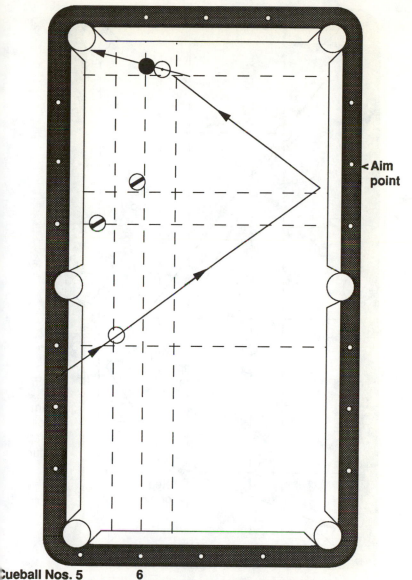

**< Aim
point**

Cueball Nos. 5   6

Advanced and Expert: The Kick Shot

Place the balls in position as shown. Align the cue stick through the center of the cue ball at the junction of the vertical and horizontal lines. Employ a firm soft stroke using force three and one half. Measure the distance from the phantom cue ball to the rubber cushion with the cue stick. Then add that amount of distance beyond the cushion. This then is the reference point used to determine the aim point. **VERIFIED**

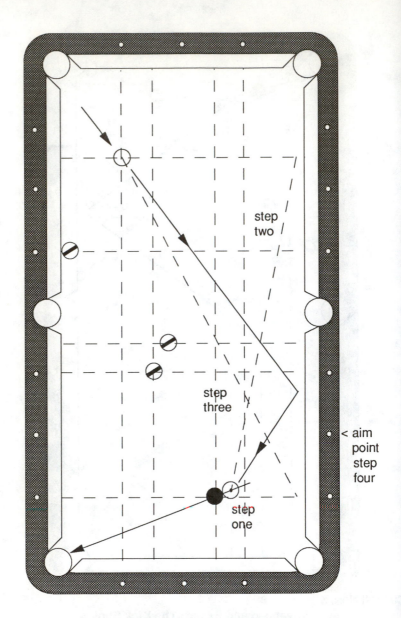

Advanced and Expert: The Kick Shot

Place the balls in position as shown. Align the cue stick through the center of the cue ball and in line with the aim point. Strike the cue ball on the vertical and horizontal center line with a moderate and firm stroke using force three. The method of computation is simple. Draw a line from the horizontal position of the cue ball at the rail contact point. Draw another line from the horizontal position of the phantom cue ball. Where the lines intersect extend a line to the rail contact position. Now draw a line from the center of the cue ball through the rail contact point onto the rail. This is the aimpoint. Object ball is 1/2 cut. VERIFIED.

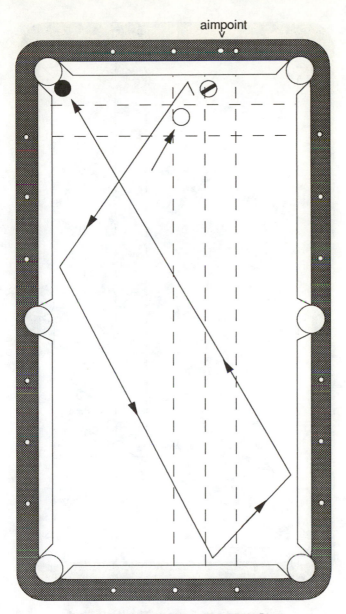

aimpoint

Advanced and Expert: The Kick Shot

Place the balls in position as shown. Align the cue stick through the center of the cue ball and in line with the aim point. Parallel that line of aim in order to strike the cue ball one cue tip below the horizontal line and one tip to the left of the vertical dividing line. Employ a firm moderate stroke using force seven. Object ball is 1/2 cut. Verified. Depends on player's ability. It is necessary to use a short follow through in order to pull the cue ball around the table.

233

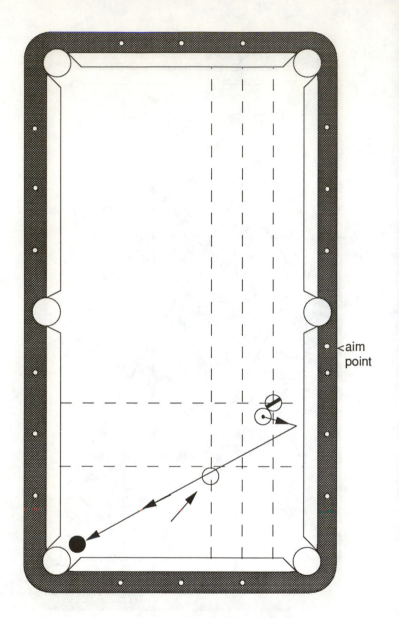

<aim
point

Advanced and Expert: The Kick Shot

Place the balls in position as shown. Align the cue stick through the center of the cue ball and in line with the aim point. Parallel that line of aim in order to strike the cue ball one half of a cue tip below the horizontal line and one half a cue tip to the right of the vertical dividing line. Employ a firm moderate stroke using force five. Object ball is 5/8 cut. VERIFIED.

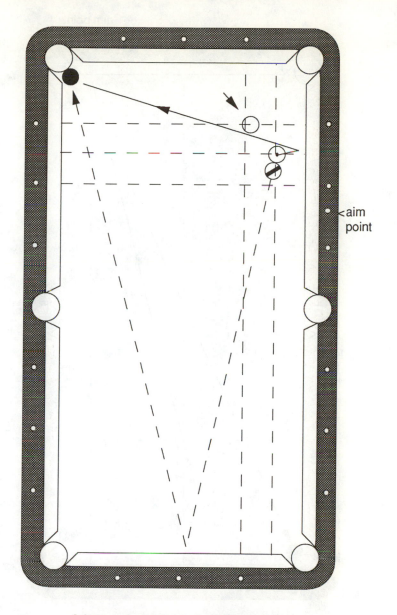

aim
point

Advanced and Expert: The Kick Shot

Place the balls in position as shown. Align the cue stick through the center of the cue ball and in line with the aim point. Parallel that line of aim in order to strike the cue ball one cue tip below the horizontal line and one and one half cue tips to the left of the vertical dividing line. Employ a firm moderate stroke using force five. Object ball is 1/8 cut. VERIFIED.

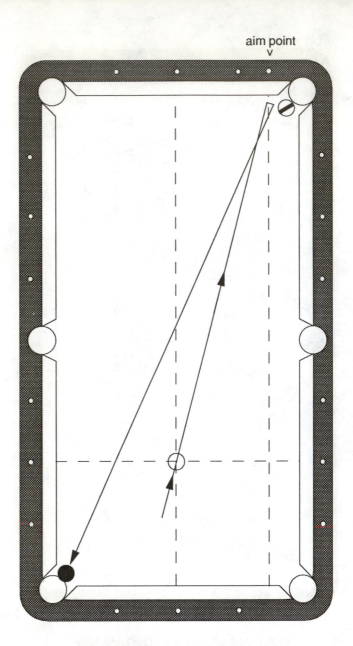

aim point

Advanced and Expert: The Kick Shot

Place the balls in position as shown. This is a judgment shot. The object is to strike the rubber cushion in front of the first object ball; then strike the first object ball at one half ball to arrive at the deflected cue ball angle required to strike the second object ball into the pocket. Strike the cue ball one cue tip below the horizontal line and one and one half a cue tips to the right of the vertical dividing line. Employ a firm moderate stroke using force six. Object ball is 1/2 cut. Verified.

236

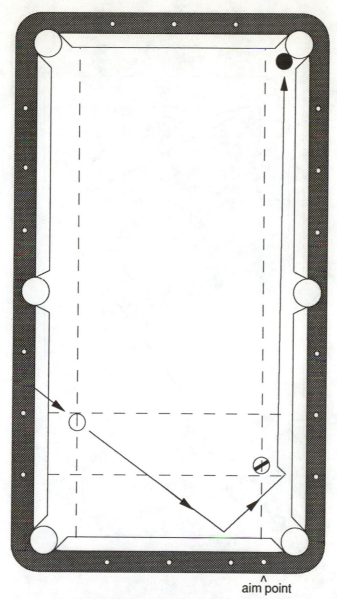

aim point

Advanced and Expert: The Kick Shot

Place the balls in position as shown. Align the cue stick through the
center of the cue ball and in line with the aim point. Parallel that line of
aim in order to strike the cue ball one half of a cue tip below the
horizontal line and one cue tip to the left of the vertical dividing line.
Employ a firm moderate stroke using force six. The first object ball is to
be struck a half ball contact after the second rail contact then the cue
ball slides towards the corner pocket. Object ball is 1/2 cut. Verified.

237

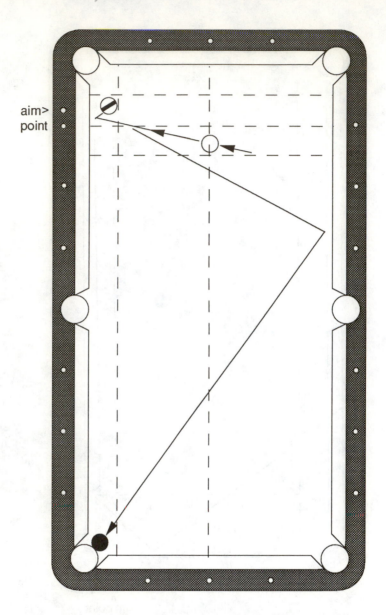

aim>
point

Advanced and Expert: The Kick Shot

Place the balls in position as shown. Align the cue stick through the center of the cue ball and in line with the aim point. Parallel that line of aim in order to strike the cue ball one cue tip above the horizontal line and one half a cue tip to the left of the vertical dividing line. Employ a firm moderate stroke using force five. The object ball is contacted at one fourth ball as measured from the return of the rail. Object ball is 1/4 cut. Verified.

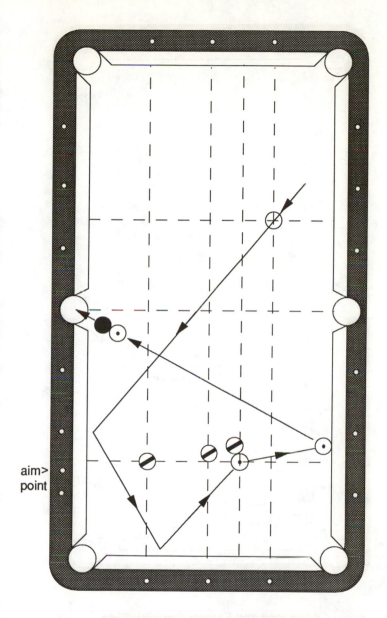

aim>
point

Advanced and Expert: The Kick Shot

Position balls as shown. Align the cue stick through the center of the cue ball and in line with the aim point. Now move the cue stick by paralleling to the left of the vertical center and above the horizontal center. Strike the cue ball with a firm moderate stroke using force five. The object here is to manufacture the "V" shape as visualized by the contact of the first two rails. From the third rail contact the cue ball will widen the angle due to the influence of the first Object ball hit. The object ball is hit full. Verified.

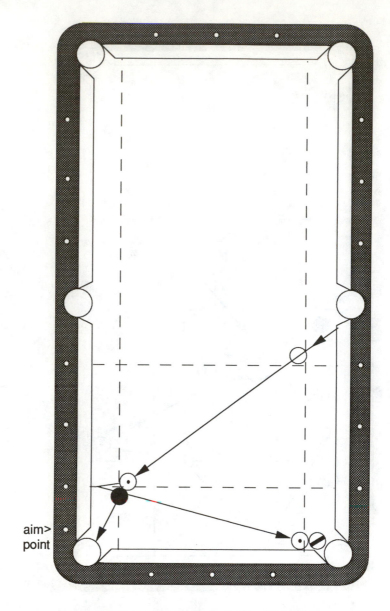

aim>
point

Advanced and Expert: The Kick Shot

Place the balls in position as shown. Align the cue stick through the center of the cue ball and in line with the aim point. Parallel the line of the cue stick to the left in order to order to strike the cue ball two cue tips or one half inch from the vertical center line. Strike the cue ball firmly with a soft stroke employing force three. The influence of english will cause the cue ball to travel from the rail on an angle to arrive at the second object ball. Object ball is 5/8 cut. Verified.

240

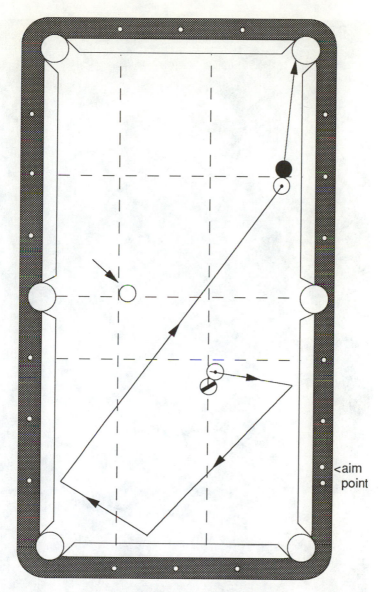

<aim
point

Advanced and Expert: The Kick Shot

Position the balls as shown. Align the cue stick through the center of the cue ball and in line with the aim point. Parallel that line of aim in order to strike the cue ball slightly below the horizontal center and one and one half cue tips to the right of the vertical dividing center. Employ a moderate stroke using force five. The cue ball should curve slightly after the cushion contact. Object ball is hit thin. Shot completion depends on skill level. Not verified but possible.

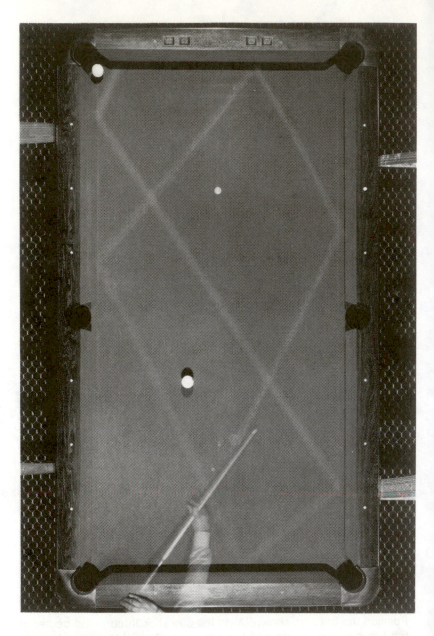

Adv. and Expert 5 rail kick #126 Raftis

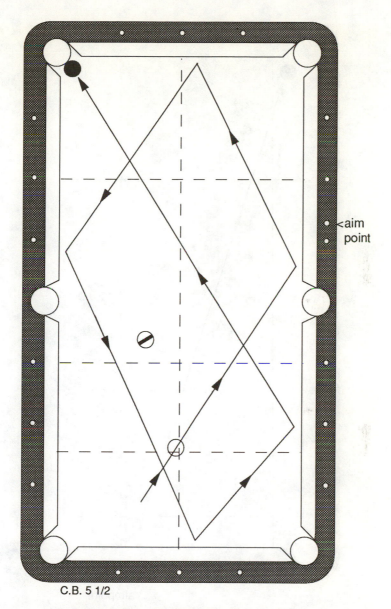

C.B. 5 1/2

Advanced and Expert: The Kick Shot

Place the cue ball on the line from cue ball position five and one half to rail position two and two thirds. Align the cue stick through the center of the cue ball and in line with the aim point. Strike the cue ball at the junction of the vertical and horizontal lines employing a hard firm stroke using force nine. Object ball is hit full. VERIFIED.

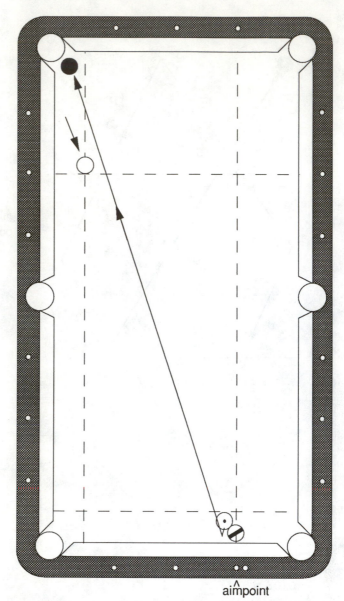

aim[^]point

Advanced and Expert: The Kick Shot

Position the balls as shown. Align the cue stick through the center of the cue ball and in line with the aim point. Parallel that line of aim in order to strike the cue ball one cue tip above the horizontal line and slightly more than one cue tip to the right of the vertical dividing line. Employ a soft stroke using force four. The cue ball should curve slightly after the cushion contact. Object ball is 1/3 cut. Verified.

Jeff Hoeksema addressing c.b.   -front view

Jeff Hoeksema prior to stroke   -front view

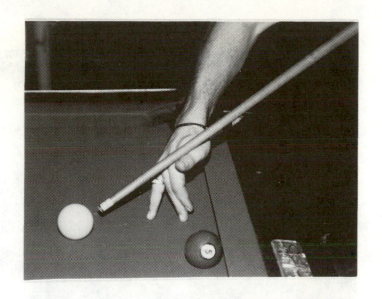

Jeff Hoeksema addressing c.b.   -side view

Jeff Hoeksema prior to stroke   -side view

247

Adv. and Expert-Jump Shot 146-B.Carson-O.H.

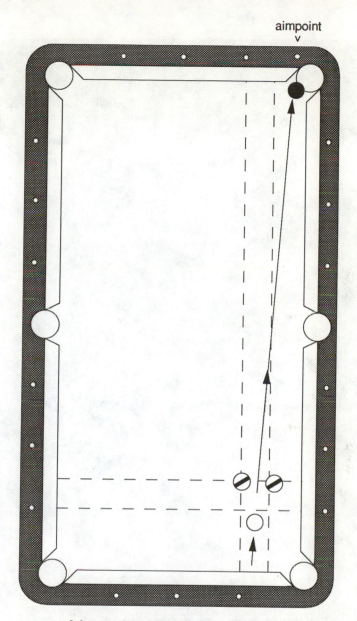

aimpoint
v

Advanced and Expert: The Jump Shot

Place balls in position as shown. Align your body and the cue stick through the center of the cue ball and in line with the aim point. Strike down on the cue ball at an angle of 45°. Strike the cue ball one cue tip above the horizontal axis line and on the vertical axis line. Employ a firm moderate stroke using force four. The cue ball will imperceptibly jump and score the object ball hit. The two obstructing balls are spaced to allow about two-thirds of the cue ball to pass through. Object ball is hit full. VERIFIED. Photo

249

Adv. and Expert-Jump Draw 119-B.Carson-O.H.

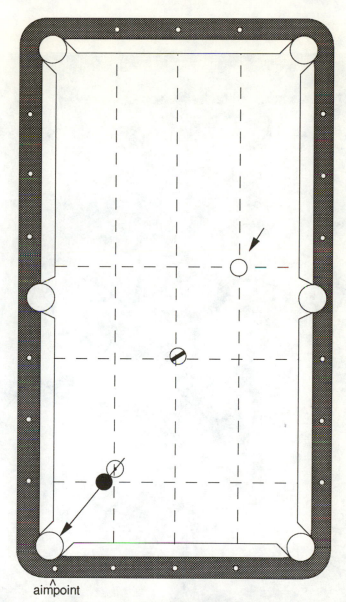

aimpoint

Advanced and Expert: The Jump Draw

Place the balls as shown. Align the cue stick through the center of the cue ball and in line with the aim point. Angle cue stick to 45°. Strike the cue ball below the horizontal axis line as viewed from cue angle by one cue tip. Employ a firm moderate stroke using force six. Object ball is 15/16 cut. Verified. Photo.

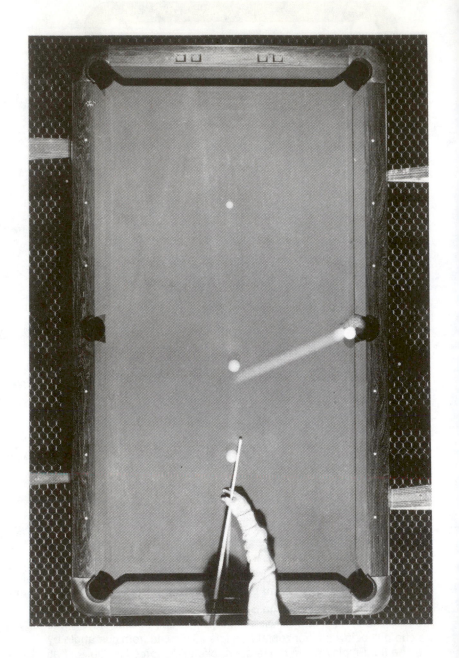

Adv. and Expert-Spinner 147-C.Raftis-O.H.

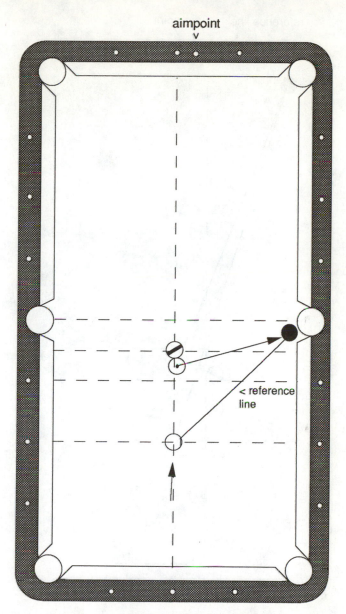

aimpoint
v

< reference
line

Advanced and Expert: The Spinner

Place balls in position as shown. Draw a reference line from the cue
ball to the object ball. Where the line contacts the cue ball indicates the
amount of spin or influence needed to produce the shot pattern. Align
the cue stick through the center of the cue ball and in line with the aim
point. Now parallel that line of aim to the right of the vertical center
dividing line by two cue tips or eight tenths of an inch. Strike the cue
ball slightly below the horizontal center with a firm stroke using force
two. The cue ball should slide to the object ball after contacting the first
ball. Object ball is 15/16 cut. VERIFIED. Photo.

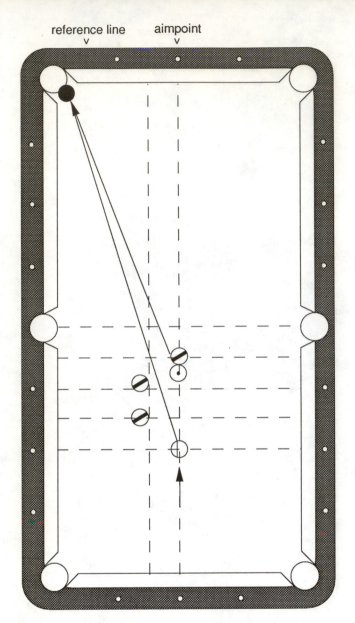

reference line   aimpoint

Advanced and Expert: The Spinner

Place balls in position as shown. Draw a reference line from the hidden object ball to the cue ball. From the point where the reference line contacts the cue ball draw a line to the opposite side of the cue ball. This intersecting line at the cue ball's surface is the amount of english or influence allotted to the cue ball. Align the cue stick through the center of the cue ball and with the aim point. Parallel that line of aim in order to strike the cue ball on the left side. Strike the cue ball above the horizontal center and to the left of the vertical center by a half of one cue tip or one quarter inch. Employ a moderate soft stroke using force three. Cue ball should follow onto the object ball. Object ball is hit full.

254   VERIFIED

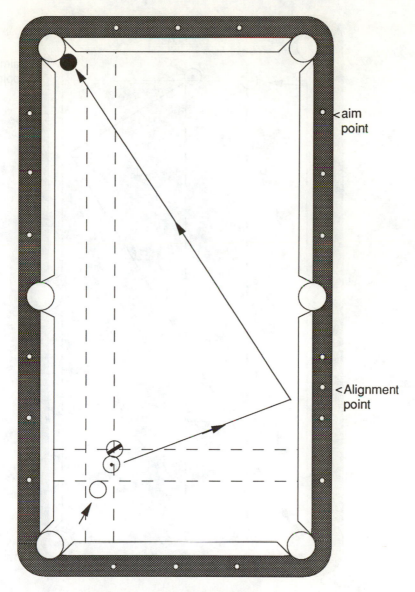

Advanced and Expert: The Spinner

Place the balls in position as shown. Align the cue stick through the center of the cue ball and in line with the aim point. Parallel the line of aim in order to strike the cue ball one half of a cue tip above center and one and one half cue tips to the left of the vertical dividing line. Employ a firm moderate stroke using force five. Object ball is 3/4 cut.

255

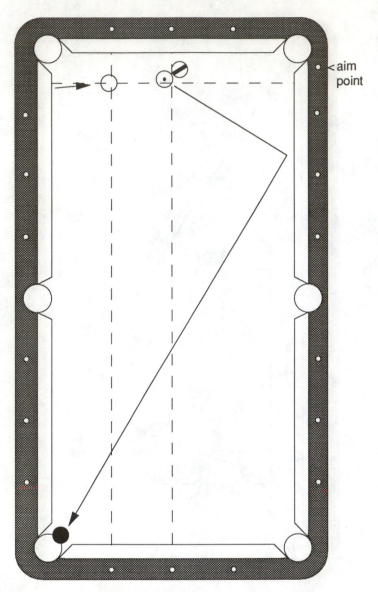

< aim point

Advanced and Expert: The Spinner

Place the balls in position as shown. Align the cue stick through the center of the cue ball and in line with the aim point. Parallel the line of aim in order to strike the cue ball one half of a cue tip above the horizontal center and one and one half cue cue tips to the right of the vertical dividing line. Strike the cue ball with a frim moderate stroke using force six. Object ball is 1/2 cut. VERIFIED

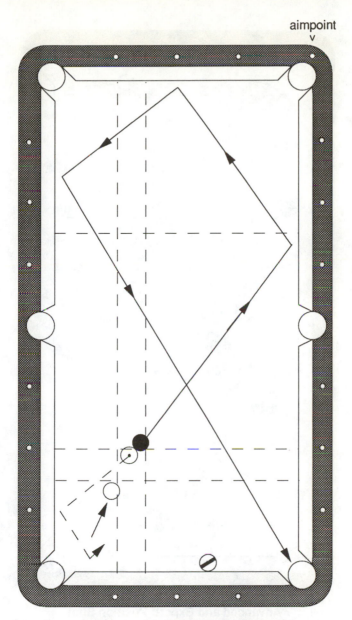

aimpoint
v

Advanced and Expert: Position Shot

Place balls in position as shown. Align the cue stick through the center of the cue ball and in line with the aim point. Parallel the line of aim in order to strike the cue ball one and one half cue tips below the horizontal dividing line and one and one half cue tips to the left of the vertical dividing line. Employ a firm moderate stroke using force six. Object ball is 7/8 cut. Verified.

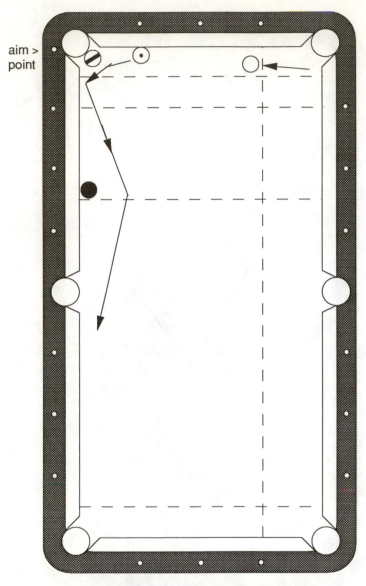

aim >
point

Advanced and Expert: Position Shot

Place the balls in position as shown. Align the cue stick through the center of the cue ball and in line with the aim point. Parallel the line of aim in order to strike the cue ball above the horizontal center and to the right of the vertical dividing line. Strike the cue ball with a firm moderate stroke using force four and one half. The cue ball will strike the rail first, pocket the first object ball and then strike the second rail. After striking the second rail, the cue ball will swerve around the second object ball and come to rest near the rail to have the second object ball straight on the pocket. Object ball is 2/3 cut. Verified.

258

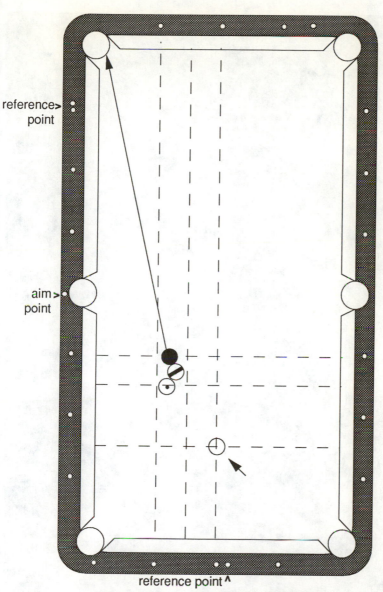

reference> point

aim > point

reference point ^

Advanced and Expert: The Throw shot

Place balls in position as shown. Align the cue stick through the center of the cue ball and in line with the aim point. Parallel the line of aim to the left in order to strike the cue ball below the horizontal center and to the left of the vertical center line one and one half cue tips. Employ a firm soft stroke using force three. Strike the object ball one eighth left. With a little practice throw shots could be a big addition to your game. Verified.

259

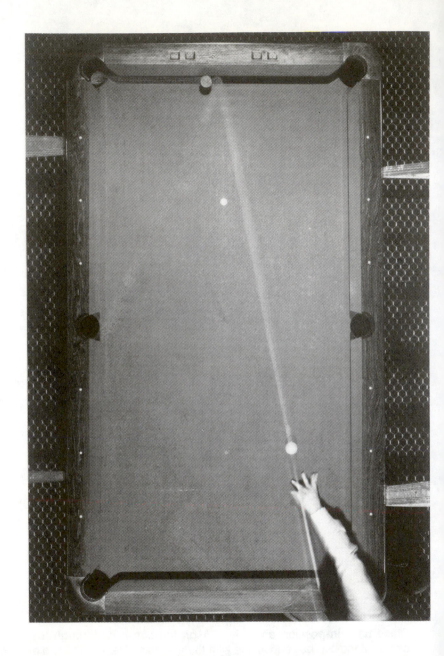

Adv. and Expert-Cut Shots 20-C. Raftis-O.H.

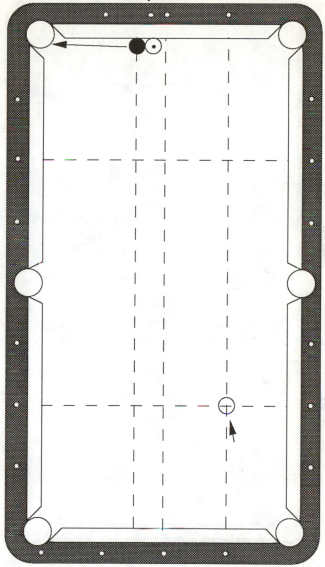

aim point

Advanced and Expert: Cut Shots

Place balls in position as shown. Align the cue stick through the center of the cue ball and in line with the aim point. Strike the cue ball above the horizontal center line and to the left of the vertical center line. Start with a one and one half cue tips of 3/4 inch inch and increase if necessary. The object is to strike the rail before striking the object ball. In other words, you hit the rail first and kick in the object ball. Employ a firm moderate stroke using force five. Verified. Photo.

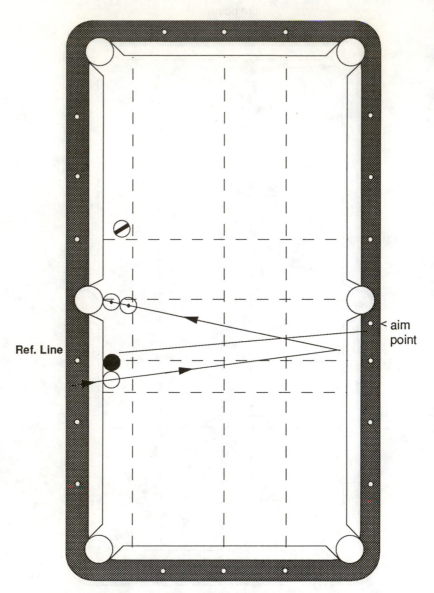

Ref. Line

aim point

Advanced and Expert: The Time Shot

Place balls in position as shown. Strike the object ball thin in order for it to be slow moving. By the time the object ball travels the distance to the pocket opening the cue ball has to travel twice across the table to meet the object ball at the pocket opening. Strike the cue ball above the horizontal center and slightly to the left of the vertical dividing line. Tap the cue ball and object ball into position and make sure that they are touching before attempting the shot. Object ball is 1/32 cut. VERIFIED

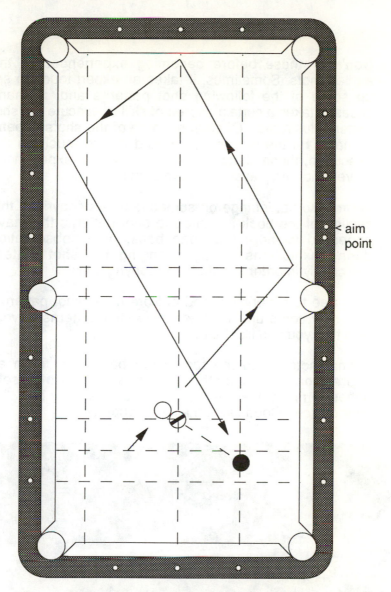

aim
point

Advanced and Expert: The Time Shot

Place balls in position as shown. Align the cue stick through the center of the cue ball and in line with the aim point. Parallel that line of aim in order to strike the cue ball one and one half cue tips below the horizontal line and one and one half cue tips to the left of the vertical dividing line. Employ a firm moderate stroke using force six. The first object ball strikes the second object ball towards the corner pocket and the cue ball travels around the table in order to kick the second object ball into the corner pocket. Object ball is 1/20 cut. Verified. This is a difficult shot pattern but a possibility.

FANCY SHOTS.

Don't try these before becoming experienced at the earlier shots. Sometimes, it takes an expert touch to set up some of the following shot patterns and, in many cases, it takes a certain degree of skill to execute the shot pattern illustrated. Of course, some of the shots depend primarily on the proper set up and not so much on the execution, these shots can be tried by an inexperienced player and the player can have some success.

In order to not infringe on someone else's copyright, this section of the book is limited to shot patterns that have appeared in more than one book, or by observation during exhibitions, or by changing the shot pattern sufficiently in order to satisfy the copyright law.

Feel free to experiment and explore these shot patterns. You may come up with a few new shot patterns of your own that you can illustrate.

A final note: Tap the top of the ball to set in in an impression in the cloth, or use a removable, self-adhesive ring binder reinforcement to locate the ball. It's your choice. Good luck on all your endeavors.

Benjamin Jardin addressing c.b.   -side view

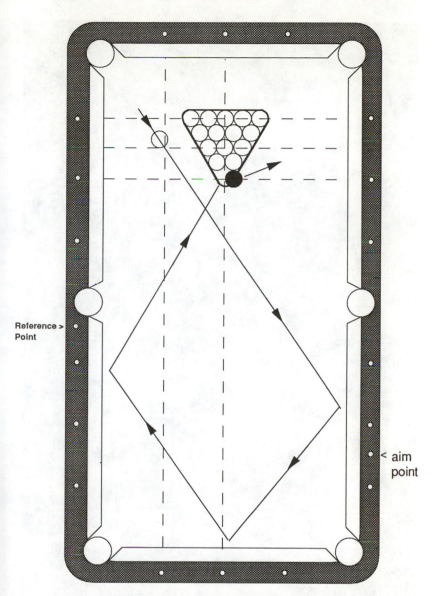

Reference >
Point

< aim
point

Beginners and Intermediates: Fancy Shots

Place the fifteen object balls in the rack on the foot spot. Remove the
one ball which should be the apex ball. Use the one ball for the cue
ball and place the cue ball in position as shown to support the rack.
The one ball travels the path shown, strikes the cue ball on the left
side, knocking the cue ball out of the rack in the direction of the arrow.
The rack then falls down trapping the one ball in the position of the
apex ball or the one balls' normal position. Strike the one ball in the
center with force four. Object ball is 1/2 cut. Verified.

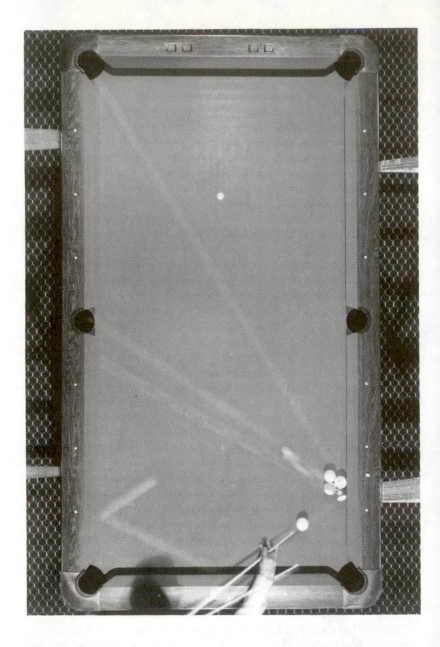

Adv. and Expert-Fancy Shots 1-C.Raftis-O.H.

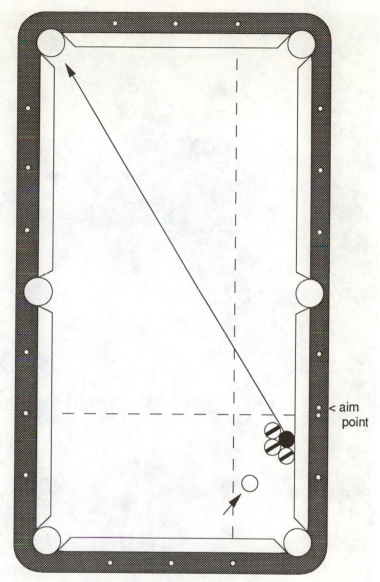

< aim
point

Advanced and Expert
Fancy Shots

Place balls in position as shown. Tap the object balls on top to imbed them into the cloth. Align the cue stick through the center of the cue ball and in line with the aim point. Strike the cue ball at the junction of the horizontal and vertical centers. Employ a firm moderate stroke using force five. Strike the first object ball straight on in order to make this shot. Verified. Photo.

267

Adv. and Expert-Fancy Shots 12-B.Carson-O.H.

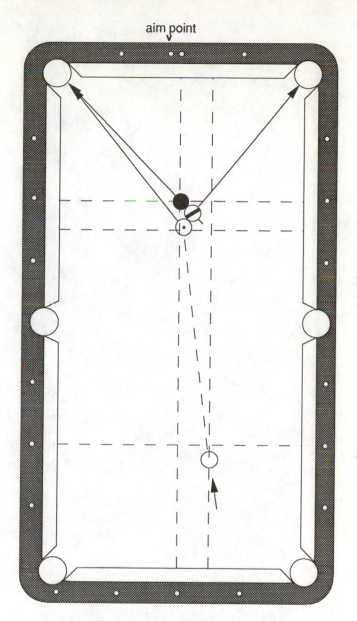

aim point

Advanced and Expert: Fancy Shots

Place the balls on the table as shown. Align the cue stick through the center of the cue ball and in line with the aim point. Strike the cue ball above the horizontal center and in line with the vertical center. Employ a firm soft stroke using force four. VERIFIED. Photo.

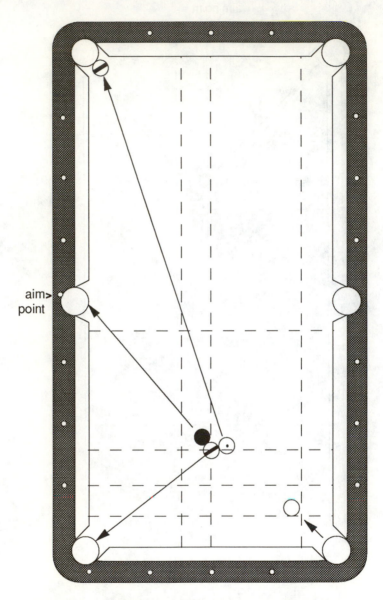

Advanced and Expert: Fancy Shots

Place the balls in position as shown. Align the cue stick through the center of the cue ball and in line with the aim point. Strike the cue ball in the center at the junctions of the vertical and horizontal dividing lines. Strike the cue ball with a firm soft stroke using force three. Remember to imbed the two object balls which are touching by tapping them on the topside with another ball. VERIFIED.

270

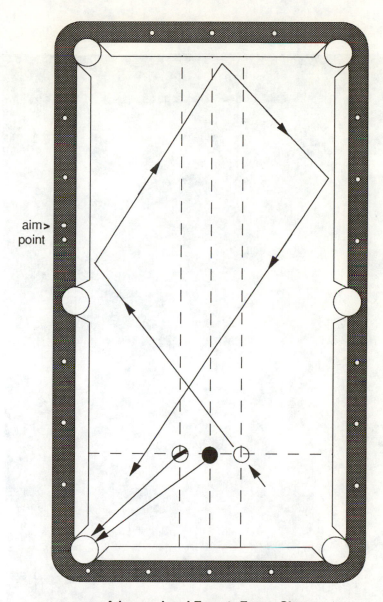

aim>
point

Advanced and Expert: Fancy Shots

Place the balls in position as shown. Align the cue stick through the center of the cue ball and with the aim point. Strike the cue ball in the center at the junctions of the vertical and horizontal lines. Strike the cue ball with a firm moderate stroke using force five and one half. Strike the second object with a soft stroke using force one. Quickly move to strike the last object ball into the pocket with a hard stroke. the idea is to pocket the last ball hit first. The second ball hit second and the first ball hit last. Verified.

271

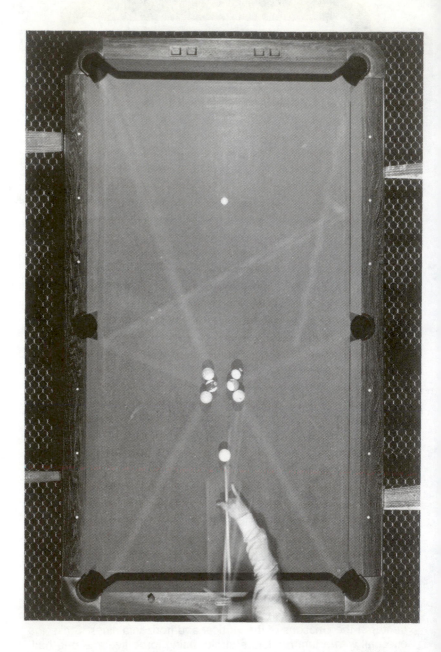

Adv. and Expert-Fancy Shots 152-C.Raftis-O.H.

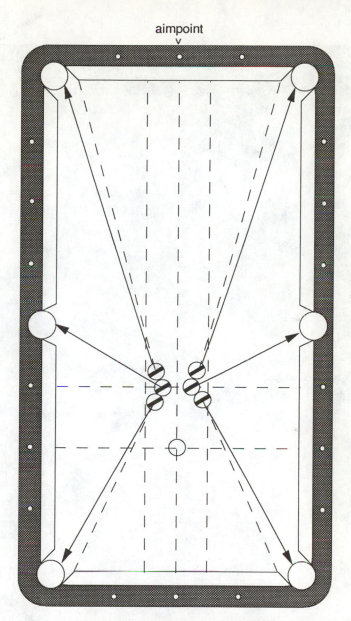

aimpoint
v

Advanced and Expert: Fancy Shots

Place balls in position as shown. Use the cue ball to tap the top of the object balls to embed them into the cloth. The two balls that enter the side pocket are spaced less than one ball apart. They also are the first balls to position. Align the cue stick through the center of the cue ball and in line with the aim point. Strike the cue ball below the horizontal center and on the vertical dividing line. Employ a firm hard stroke using force six. Both object balls are 1/20 cut. Verified. Photo.

273

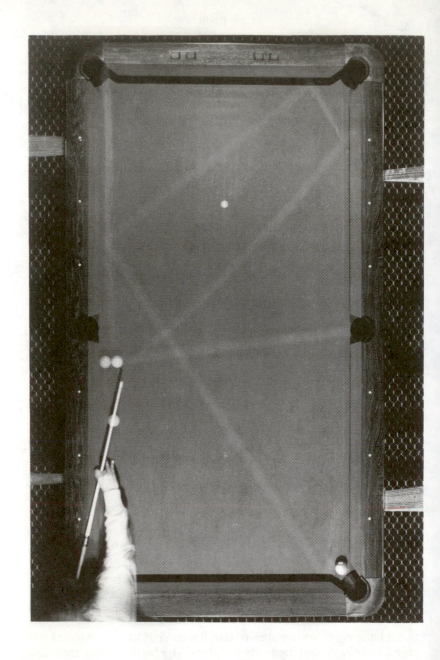

Adv. and Expert-Fancy Shots 151-Raftis-O.H.

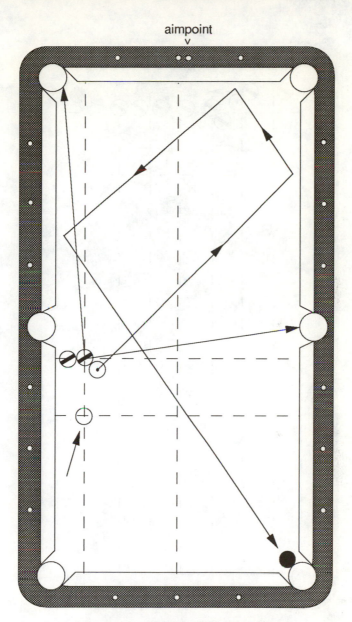

aimpoint

Advanced and Expert: Fancy Shots

Place balls in position as shown. Tap the object balls on top to imbed them in the cloth. Make sure that the two object balls are touching. Align the cue stick through the center of the cue ball and in line with the aimpoint. Parallel the line of aim in order to strike the cue ball above the horizontal center and one half cue tip to the left of the vertical center. Employ a firm moderate stroke using force six. Object ball is 1/4 cut. Verified.

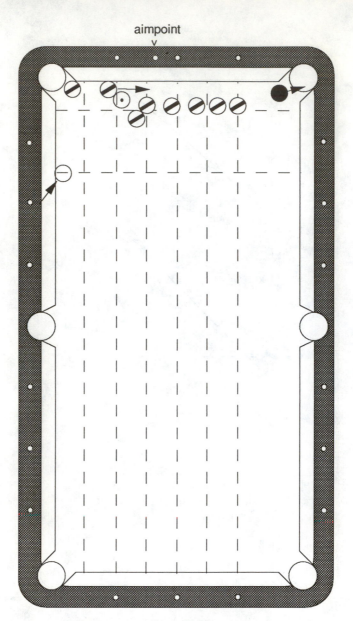

aimpoint

Advanced and Expert: Fancy Shots

Place balls in position as shown. The first object ball is on the rail and is struck so that the cue ball runs down the rail to pocket number five. The other object balls are placed less than one ball distant from the rubber cushion. Align the cue stick through the center of the cue ball and in line with the aim point. Strike the cue ball above the horizontal center and to the right of the vertical dividing line. Use a firm moderate stoke using force five. This is known as the machine gun shot for the fast sound clicks it makes. Object ball is 1/2 cut. Verified.

276

aimpoint

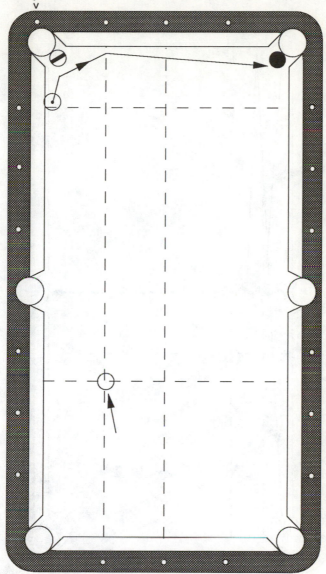

Advanced and Expert: Fancy Shots

Place ball in position as shown. Align the cue stick through the center of the cue ball and in line with the aim point. Parallel the line of aim in order to strike the cue ball above the horizontal center and one and one half cue tips to the left of the vertical dividing line. When striking the cue ball above the horizontal center end the stroke on an upswing. Strike the cue ball with a firm soft stroke using force four. The cue ball strikes the rail in front of the first object ball then pockets the first object ball then swerves back to the rail to pocket the second object ball. Object ball is 2/3 cut. Verified.

277

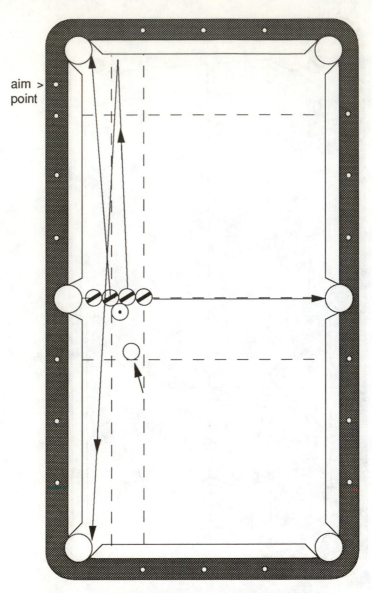

aim >
point

Advanced and Expert: Fancy Shots

Place balls in position as shown. Tap the object balls on the top to imbed them in the cloth and to make sure that they are frozen or touching one another. Align the cue stick through the center of the cue ball and in line with the aim point. Strike the cue ball at the horizontal dividing line and one and one half cue tips to the right of the vertical dividing line. Employ a firm moderate stroke using force five. Strike the third object ball from pocket number three first. Remember practice makes perfect if you practice the right principles. You may have to try this shot several times before reaching perfection. Object ball is 1/3 cut. Verified.

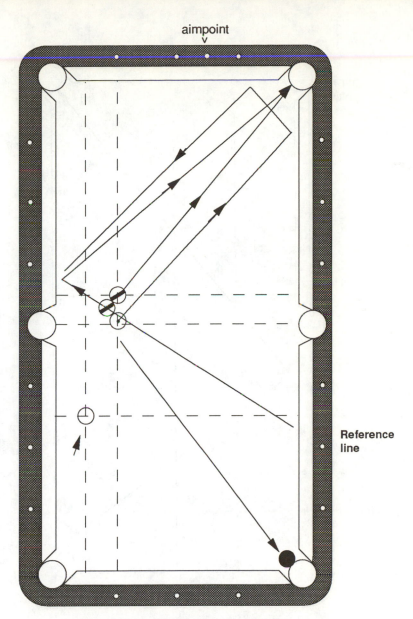

aimpoint

Reference line

Advanced and Expert: Fancy Shots

Place balls in position as shown. Align the cue stick through the center of the cue ball and in line with the aim point. Parallel that line of aim in order to strike the cue ball to the left of the vertical center line one and one half cue tips and above the horizontal dividing line. Strike the cue ball with a firm moderate stroke using force six. Strike the first object ball one fourth on the right. On all fancy shots imbed the object ball and make sure that they are touching one another. Object ball is 1/4 cut. Verified.

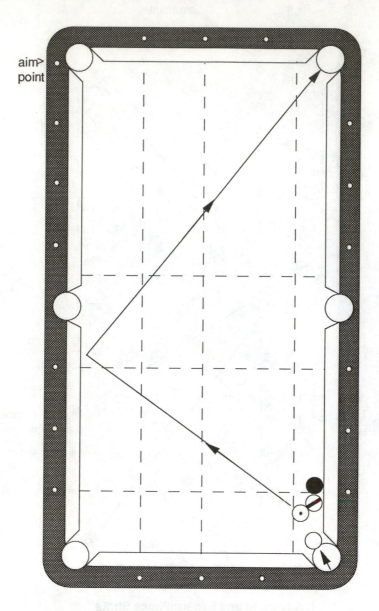

Advanced and Expert: Fancy Shots

Place the balls in position as shown. Align the cue stick through the center of the cue ball and in line with the aim point. Parallel the line of aim in order to strike the cue ball slightly below the horizontal center and to the right of the vertical center. Employ a firm soft stroke using force four. The purpose of this shot is to have the cue ball meet and contact the second object ball just in front of the pocket in order to pocket the second object ball into pocket five. This is a time shot. The timing must be perfect. Object ball is 1/2 cut. Verified.

COMPETITION.

IN ORDER TO COMPETE YOU MUST BE MENTALLY AND PHYSICALLY PREPARED. To be mentally prepared you need to be able to concentrate, which means to place only one thought or object in the mind's eye at one time. Mental discipline is required. This can be obtained by mental exercises such as adding numbers mentally instead of physically. There are other mental exercises such as remembering or memorizing shot patterns. Mental stability is necessary, which means that you should be peaceful and your home situation should be stable. The ability to make good judgements is necessary. These judgements are based on experiences. You must be mentally alert and attentive. Physically you should have stamina and good eyesight. You should be comfortable and not tense. You must be determined to win or play your best. Patience is a virtue worth cultivating. When your opponent is shooting, the only thing that you can do is wait and be patient. You must stay composed and not become disturbed while awaiting your turn at the table. And even while playing you do not want to become disturbed by missed shots or scratches. In other words you should be at your best performance while competing; both mentally and physically.

STRATEGY: Before you can plan your strategy, you need to know your opponents' weak and strong points. Following are several profiles of different player's styles:

A. AN AGGRESSIVE PLAYER. An aggressive player will shoot at all shots. This player is very difficult to defeat when he is on his game. Seeing that he will shoot at anything you may be able to turn the game around by playing deliberate safeties. These safeties will tend to slow him down plus give you some scoring opportunities. Leave the aggressive player many long thin shots, snookers, or balls frozen against a cushion.

B. NEXT IS THE SAFETY PLAYER. A safety player will not shoot out. If the shot is not a high percentage shot then the safety player will play a deliberate safety. In order to defeat such a player you will also have to play safeties. You cannot shoot out at low percentage shots, because this would tire you out and give your opponent better scoring opportunities. So play safe; leave your opponent snookered, or with a ball against a cushion, or a long thin cut shot.

C. THE DETERMINED PLAYER. The determined player will score a few balls then play safe. Again he will score a few balls and play safe. It is very difficult to defeat a determined player. Your only strategy is to run out the rack or play him at his own game. In other words you make a few balls and play safe. This may unnerve your opponent. If the opportunity arises, go for the run out. Sometimes your best defense is a strong offense.

D. AND NOW THE FRONT RUNNER. The front runner tries to get in front quickly and then increase the lead by taking risks at scoring. The front runner is almost impossible to defeat. He is a shoot out player and if you want to compete it is best to compete on his level. It is possible to slow him down or put him off his game by playing deliberate safeties. This is time consuming and if you are not an excellent safety player then it may be to no avail.

E. THE HUSTLER OR POOL SHARP. The hustler never shows his true strength. He tries to "milk" the game. In other words he will try to take an advantage by winning two out of three or three out of five games. He tries to gain an advantage over a period of time. If you know that you are being hustled, it is best to minimize your losses by quitting or increase your opportunities by increasing the spot. One way to identify a hustler is that he may consistently come from behind by running out the last balls on the table. Another way is that most of his shots are lucky shots. In other words the object ball may be almost straight in the corner but he will play it three rails into a different pocket and if it goes in he will say "what good luck". Also he may miss some easy shots and leave you safe so that you will again leave him an easy shot.

PRACTICAL ADVICE:

A. YOU HAVE TO BE PEACEFUL. You cannot be easily disturbed. You need to have patience. You need to persevere. In other words the game is not over until the last shot is completed. Or the match is not over until the last game is won. You need to concentrate on the immediate shot. Picture the completed shot in your mind. Predetermine the force of the stroke and where the cue ball will be left. Play the object ball for the correct entry into the pocket. Try to have only one thought in your mind at one time. You have to believe in your own success.

B. YOU MUST PRACTICE ON A REGULAR BASIS. Try to always increase your percentage of completion on the different shot patterns. Unusual shots also need to be practiced. Practice force control. Remember when cutting an object ball that the less the object ball is contacted, the more the speed of the cue ball. Begin by practicing one half hour a day and then try to increase to two hours a day. One eye will coordinate the body with the shot at hand. Let the right eye be predominate if you are left handed and let the left eye be predominate if you are right handed.

PLAN AHEAD

Try to make a plan when reading the table. In other words try to determine the sequence of shots that you plan to make mentally. After making a determination then try to execute your plan. Remember in executing your plan to concentrate on making only one shot at a time. If you always make the next shot then you will successfully make all the shots. Try to visualize your plan. Look for the pictures in the mind. Of course the mind needs to be trained to see the right pictures. It is necessary when executing a shot pattern to put a little more energy into a proper execution to ensure proper position. Don't just pocket the object ball without considering the position of the cue ball for the next shot.

FOOD INTAKE:

Don't eat a heavy meal prior to the start of a match. A heavy meal can cause sluggish reactions. Try to consume a light meal or take several small amounts of food instead. This will keep the body light and the mind alert. For some players light refreshments could be only liquids or hard candies. Fasting from foods may increase mental awareness. Try to refrain from smoking and ask your opponent to not smoke at the table. This will reduce irritations to the eyes and throat. Also smoking by yourself or others can help to break your concentration on the immediate shot pattern.

PERSONAL ATTITUDE:

The attitude that you should have towards your opponent is that you are engaged in a test or a battle and that your opponent is your enemy. That doesn't mean that your opponent is always your enemy. It means that your opponent is your enemy during the contest. You don't want to think harshly about him. You want to realize that here is a battle and this is my opponent. He is my enemy and I want to do whatever is in my power to defeat him.

Always be a gentleman or woman and be serious about playing the game of pool. Pool can be a lot of fun but it also can be a lot of hard work. Use your turn at the table for your best advantage. Try to minimize your mistakes. Usually the player who makes the most mistakes loses and the player making the least mistakes wins. You should always endeavor to win every game and every match.

Your opponent may be your teacher or a friend, but when the game starts you must take an impersonal attitude toward your opponent and try to win the match. You have to think that you have to win every game and make every shot. Always try to defeat your opponent by not letting him have a good shot or win even one game.

WHAT SHOULD BE YOUR ATTITUDE TOWARDS A CROWD? If the crowd is friendly then that is to your advantage and you should enjoy a pleasing attitude. If there is a heckler in the crowd then you should develop an impersonal attitude. Remember that every turn at the table is an opportunity to win and if you concentrate on your winning strategy, then you will not notice the heckler or you will be able to minimize the attitude of the heckler.

An unfriendly crowd is one that is favorable towards your opponent. Here again the impersonal attitude has to come into play. Try to concentrate on the shot at hand and play one shot at a time. Try to show confidence in your game. Don't become upset or irritated towards an unfriendly crowd. Remember that these times will pass and if you perform well the crowd may turn in your favor.

Dominic Zito addressing cue ball   -front view

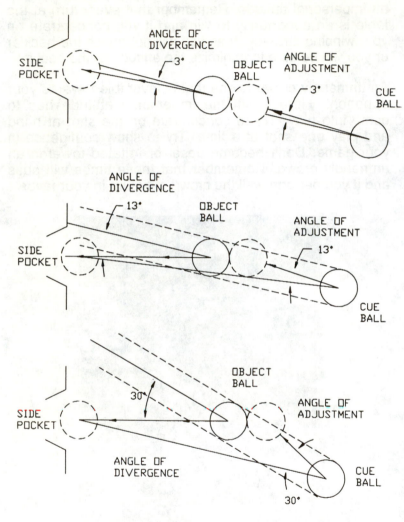

Examples of angle of deviation equals angle of adjustment

HELPFUL ADVICE.

STUDY LONG AND YOU STUDY WRONG.

When you first approach the table and read the table, you will make judgements. After making these judgements, you have to be determined not to change your mind. First you visualize making the shots and then you execute the shots. Don't make plans and then keep changing them.

DIFFERENT STROKES FOR DIFFERENT FOLKS.

No one player plays exactly like another. It can be explained to you why you should play a shot in a certain way and it can be explained why one method may be better than another but ultimately it is up to you to determine your style of play.

WIPE OR BRUSH THE CHALK ONTO THE CUE TIP.

Place the chalk on the cue tip as an abrasive for contact with the cue ball. It is not necessary to chalk the cue tip for every shot but it is recommended to chalk the cue tip often. By grinding the chalk onto the cue tip, you may remove more chalk than you put on which defeats the purpose of the chalk.

IF YOU THINK THAT YOU SHOULD PLAY A SAFETY THEN PLAY A SAFETY.

You have to be decisive even if your decision is wrong. When it's your turn at the table and you read the table and decide that the best shot is a safety then play the best safety that you can play.

MISS THE SHOT ON THE PROFESSIONAL SIDE OF THE POCKET.

You should play a shot pattern for the proper entrance into the pocket. For long angle shots into the corner pocket you have to especially avoid hitting the long rail before the pocket opening. For side pocket shots and for short angle shots you have to avoid hitting the nearest corner.

HERE IS A SPECIAL PROCEDURE FOR CUT SHOTS.

When the cue ball and the object ball are both in a line with a desired pocket, in other words a straight in shot, you aim the cue stick through the center of the cue ball and in line with the center of the pocket. A point in the pocket then becomes the target. By aiming at a point in the pocket the object ball will automatically enter the pocket. It is relatively easier to aim the cue ball for the pocket opening than it is to try to pick a spot on the object ball to strike or to aim to cover the object ball with the cue ball.

HERE IS ANOTHER PROCEDURE FOR CUT SHOTS.

Another procedure is when the object ball is slightly out of line with the cue ball and the desired pocket then it is only necessary to adjust the alignment for the cue stick for the amount or degree of deviation of the alignment.

HERE IS A SPECIAL PROCEDURE FOR PLAYING POSITION.

When the object ball is close to a desired pocket opening, then you may cut the object ball into one side of the pocket or the other which would be determined by the position of the second desired object ball. Normally the pocket opening is more than two balls wide which allows for some leaway when playing the shot for position. Take advantage of this easy opportunity to play position by not shooting the object ball straight into the pocket.

ALWAYS TRUST YOUR FIRST JUDGEMENT.

Your mind can be your worst enemy or your best friend. Train your mind by reading the table and knowing your ability to score, then this information will come forward when you analyze the shot patterns. Trust your own experience and judgement.

ALWAYS ACKNOWLEDGE A GOOD SCORING OPPORTUNITY.

Sometimes the object ball is on a line from the center of the pocket and the pocket opening, which means that you have the maximum scoring opportunity. When you have a wide angle entry into the pocket then your scoring opportunity is much greater than a small narrow angle of entry.

PROFIT BY YOUR OPPONENTS MISTAKES.

This is generally the difference between winning and losing. If two players are of equal strengths then the player who doesn't make mistakes or who profits by his opponents' mistakes will win the game and the match.

MAKE THE SHOT PATTERN CLEAN.

In other words do not make shots where the ball bounces back and forth in the pocket opening and then falls into the pocket. In other words do not touch the rail edge in front of the pocket or the corner of the pocket which would then cause the object ball to wobble before dropping into the pocket. Another fault is to over stroke the cue ball or apply an exceptional force to the cue ball, this may cause the object ball to bounce back and forth in the pocket opening or to enter the pocket and then come back out.

THE DEEPER THE CUSHION INDENTION THE SMALLER THE ANGLE OF REBOUND.

This information can help you to make bank and kick shots when the balls are slightly out of line with the reference angle. Also this information can help you to make your bank and kick shots by helping to teach you to play the right speed for the desired shot pattern.

ONCE THE CUE BALL IS STRUCK THE SHOT IS FINISHED.

No amount of contortions or leaning will influence the shot after the cue ball has been struck. By leaning your body or your cue stick you cannot influence the shot that is in progress. You have to do everything correctly before striking the cue ball. If you have executed the shot properly then nothing your opponent can do will stop the shot from scoring.

PLAY HALF SAFETIES.

If you do not think that you can score or if you have not been getting a good percentage on a shot pattern or if your opponent has not left you a good shot, then play a half safety. A half safety is when you try to make a shot but knowing that the shot pattern is not likely to produce the best result, you plan to leave the cue ball or the object ball in a difficult position for your opponent. In other words you try to score but you adjust the speed of the ball so that in case you miss your opponent will not be left with a set up or an easy shot.

PRACTICE MAKES PERFECT.

Practice makes perfect only if you practice the right concepts. First you must accept good instruction then you practice accomplishing that instruction. It is the author's judgement that this book offers good instruction and that by following these instructions you will advance to the expert category.

Ball Pos. at Rail-Soft Hit-C.Raftis-Front View

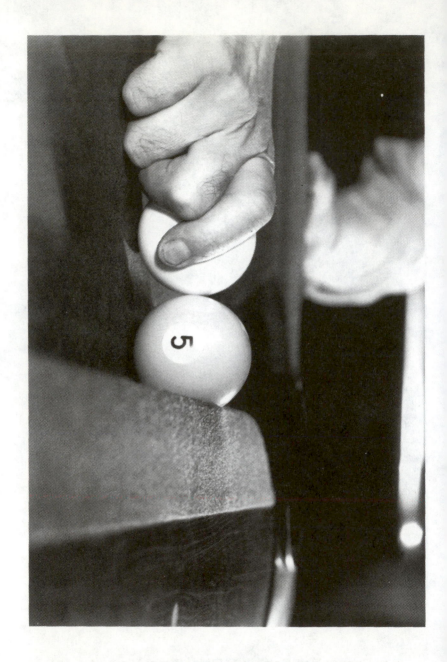

Ball Pos. at Rail-Hard Hit-C.Raftis-Frt. View

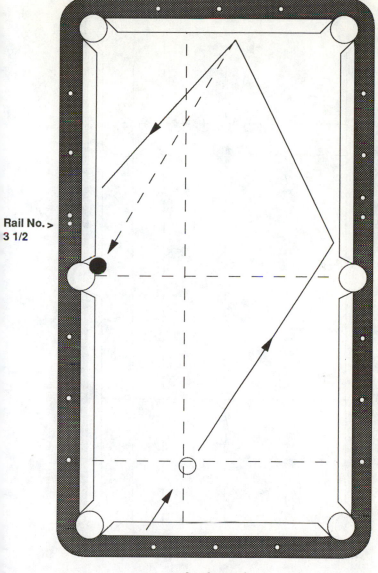

Rail No. >
3 1/2

Angle study

Place cue ball on the reference line as shown. Align the cue stick
through the center of the cue ball and in line with the aim point. Strike
lthe cue ball in the center at the junction of the vertical and horizontal
and vertical dividing lines. Strike the cue ball with just enough force to
reach pocket number three; approximately force three and one half.
The natural rebound angle would take you to three and one twelfth.

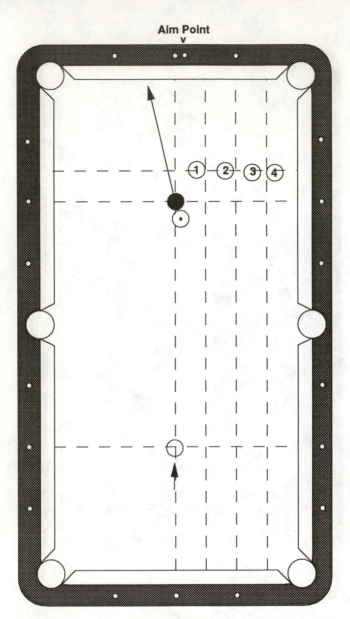

Force study

Place the balls in position as shown. Align the cue stick through the center of the cue ball and in line with the aim point. Strike the cue ball one half of cue tip below center. Always strike the object ball in the same place seven eighths right. For cue position one, use force two. For cue position two, use force four. For cue position three, use force six. And for cue ball position four use force eight.

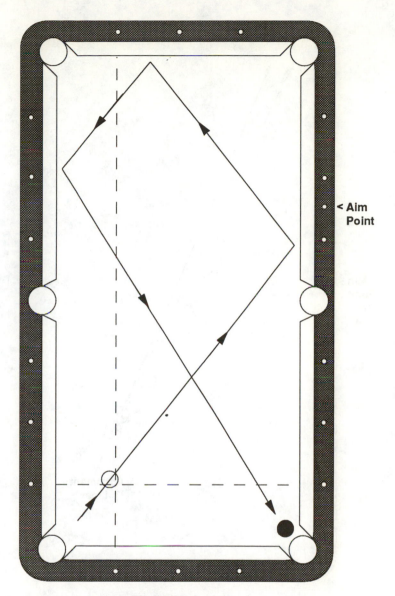

< Aim
Point

Big Ball Principle

When the object ball is near the corner pocket as shown. The
possibilities of scoring are the highest than when the object ball is
located to one side or the other of the pocket. There is approximately a
three ball wide path by the cue ball coming into the object ball. Also if
the cue ball by error of calculation arrives near the object ball on a long
or short path and contacts the rail before the object ball then there is
still the possibility to score. In other words if you miss making the
intended shot you might still pocket the object ball.

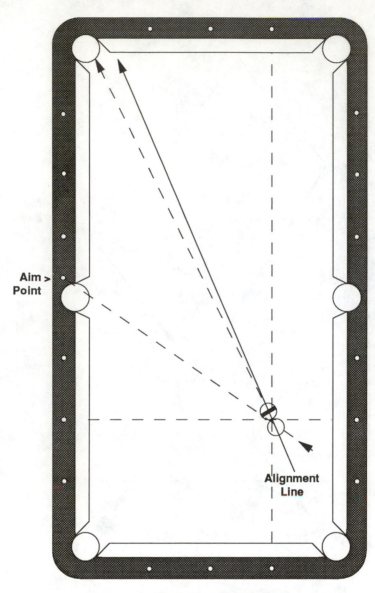

Push Shot Principle

1. Place object ball and cue ball in position as shown.
2. Strike cue ball with a center ball hit and medium speed in the direction of the number three pocket.
3. Object ball will travel along line to number four pocket

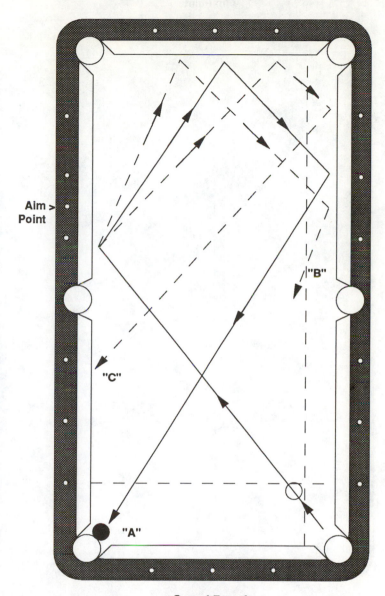

Speed Practice

Place the center of the cue ball on the reference line. To make the cue ball enter pocket number two. Strike the cue ball in the center and use force six. To make the cue ball arrive at point "C", strike the cue ball in the center and use force nine. To make the cue ball arrive at point "B", strike the cue ball in the center and use force three.

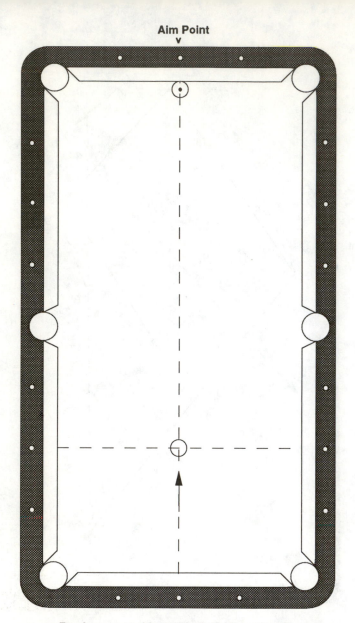

Aim Point

Beginners and Intermediate: Practice Shot

Place the the cue ball on the table as shown. Strike the cue ball in the center at the junction of the vertical and horizontal dividing lines. Employ a firm moderate stroke using forces five to six. If the cue ball is struck accurately then the cue ball will travel up and down the center line of the table without deviating. Hold the cue stick level and do not move your body until the cue ball has contacted the first rubber cushion. Visualize any deviation and make necessary corrections. VERIFIED.

ABOUT THE AUTHOR.

The author, Christos E. Raftis, was born in Indianapolis, Indiana, on March the first in the year nineteen hundred and thirty. At the age of a few months he was transported to Detroit, Michigan. While an infant his mother would leave him on the front pool table in a commercial pool hall while she went shopping. One of the first jobs he held was as a rack boy in a pool room in Mitchell, Indiana at the age of fourteen. One of his acquaintances, Bud Chastain, was also a rack boy. One pay day Bud asked Chris to play nine ball. So a game was started and at the end of a few hours , Bud had all of Chris's pay in his pocket. This led to a determination by Chris to learn how to play pool well. After about six months Chris was an improved player and was allowed to play on the front snooker table. It was a narrow pocketed table with rounded corners and Chris soon became expert. One Saturday Chris played continously for twenty six hours. He finally stopped when his mother, Lula Belle, came and stood outside the pool room and waited for him. At the age of fifteen, Chris was able to defeat all comers and especially the travelling professionals.

When Chris was sixteen, he managed Lowell Isom's pool room. Lowell was a distant cousin of Chris's on his mothers side and was allowed certain liberties with the cash in the cash register. Chris earned a good wage and along with his daily winnings and school allowance, he was one of the flushest people in town. One time after filling all his pockets with cash, he entertained three young ladies by taking them by taxi to a steak dinner in a town thirty five miles distant and then taking them all home to their houses.

After high school, Chris joined his father in Detroit, Michigan. There he played snooker at the Park Avenue Recreation and learned to play three cushion billiards at the Detroit Recreation. He was an acquaintance of Bob Mullins, Jake Bobsy, Harry Rott, Frank Labes, Jake Akrom, and Jack Fouracres. He also knew all the local hustlers as once in a while he would travel to other pool rooms and play nine ball. At that time Babyface, The Kid, and the Doc were among the local nine ball hustlers.

Chris defeated Jake Ankrom, who was a five time national champion in three cushion, at three cushion billiards one afternoon at the Park Avenue Recreation. At the time Jake was a professional instructor at the Detroit Athletic Club. Soon afterwards Chris defeated Jean La Rue who claimed to be the World's Best one armed player. Chris challenged Jean to a game of snooker and defeated him by six hundred and thirty points. Jean gave up his exhibition tour and became a counselor at Boy's Town.

In the Detroit City Championships for three cushion billiardists, Chris led Frank Labes, who was a five time national winner, thirty six to nine going to fifty. As Frank enjoyed travelling to the nationals, Chris relinquished the match to facilitate Frank's options.

During Chris's tour of duty in Kyoto, Japan during the Korean campaign, Chris in cooperation with the USO helped establish three billiard recreation centers.

Three Gratzer brothers were national Boys Club champions from Bedford, Indiana. One day while visiting his family members in Mitchell, which was ten miles south of Bedford, Chris took time off for a visit to one of Bedford's pool rooms. There he found the oldest Gratzer brother and after making a game, he won all the sets while the oldest Gratzer brother failed to win even one game. The youngest Gratzer brother witnessed his brother's failure and took up the challenge, but Chris refused to play him.

Later in nineteen hundred and sixty three, Chris was managing a large billiard lounge for George Rood in Dayton, Ohio. He was also giving free instructions; defeating most of the local players; and doing a little hustling on the side. Chris's hustle was that he would play any two amateur players at nine ball. Chris would shoot every third shot and let the two amateur players follow one another giving each other advice. Chris would win a majority of games and as the odds were two to one, he would end up winning the bets. At this time Chris learned how to play "jacked up pool"; which means that he would play with one hand holding the cue stick in the air. This was the year that Eddie Taylor, the Knoxville Bear, won the nine ball championship in Johnson City, Illinois. After winning, Eddie and one of his associates decided to travel to the different pool rooms and try to take on the local challengers. When Eddie came to Dayton Chris challenged him to a "freeze out", in other words to place the total bet on one set of games, on a race to eleven in nine ball playing "jacked up". The rule was that if any part of the cue stick would touch the table it was a foul and loss of turn. Chris defeated Eddie eleven to six; he didn't have a chance.

A few years later Chris was back in Detroit and he produced a newpaper syndication series headed up by the Detroit News, one of America's leading newspapers. The series was Cue Tips and a small booklet of fifty four pages was offered with a tag ad. The first week the ad ran, eight hundred books were sold. Soon after that Chris produced the Stroh Brewery's sports libraries pool booklet of one hundred sixty five thousand copies. These were distributed freely along with the purchase of a six pack. It was a beautiful five color presentation and the art work came from the newspaper series..

Lately Chris has been conducting free clinics in pool for the disabled and others. Also recently he gave free private lessons for four months at Pointe Billiards in Detroit, Michigan. He has won the last three national eight ball championships for thewheelchair veterans. He has also published two books on pool called "Cue Tips". One was one hundred and twenty seven pages and the other was one hundred and eighty six pages. Currently Chris is completing this book of three hundred eighty four pages with two hundred photographs, one hundred and eighty five diagrams, and approximately twenty illustrations.

Here are some tips on playing "jacked up". Hold the cue firmly just behind the balance point (this allows the cue tip to be down). Press the cue forward from an angle of thirty degrees for most shots. If you want to draw the cue ball then you have to hold the cue level with the table bed and strike the cue ball below the horizontal center with a frog kick stroke. Try to maintain contact with the cue ball as long as possible unless it is a short draw where you need to remove the cue stick quickly. It is also possible to hold the cue above the head and sight down the inside of the cue for aligning a shot. These shot patterns take practice and it's best to become expert at the fundamentals before trying "jacked up" pool.

Finally may all your shots make and may you win all your games.

Author playing jacked-up-C.Raftis

Jacked up-Cue under chin-C.Raftis-Front View

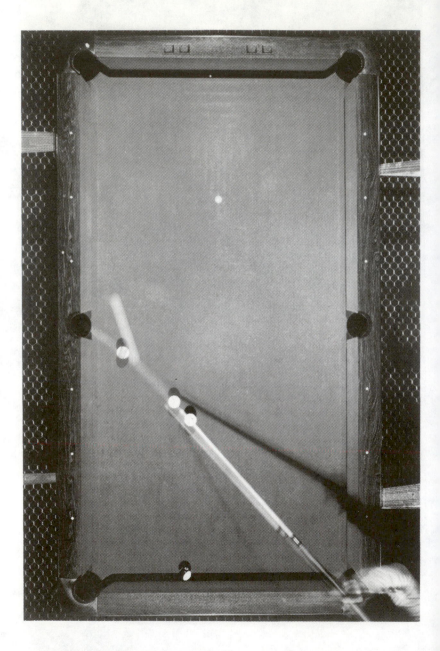

Jacked up-Cue over head- C.Raftis-Top View

Jacked up-Cue over head-C.Raftis-Front View

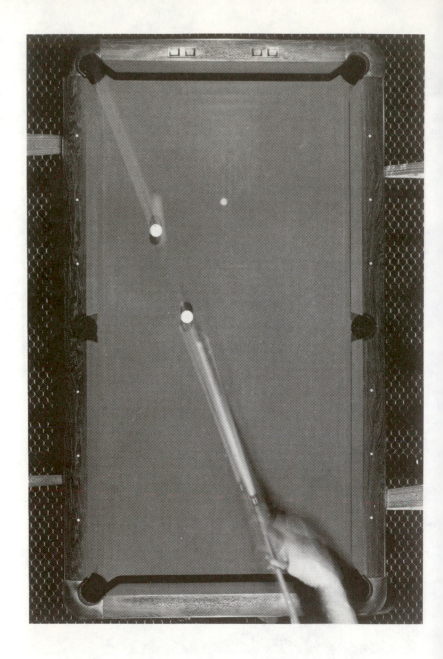

Jacked up-Frog Kick Stroke-C.Raftis-O.H.

Jacked up-Frog Kick Stroke-C.Raftis-Frt View

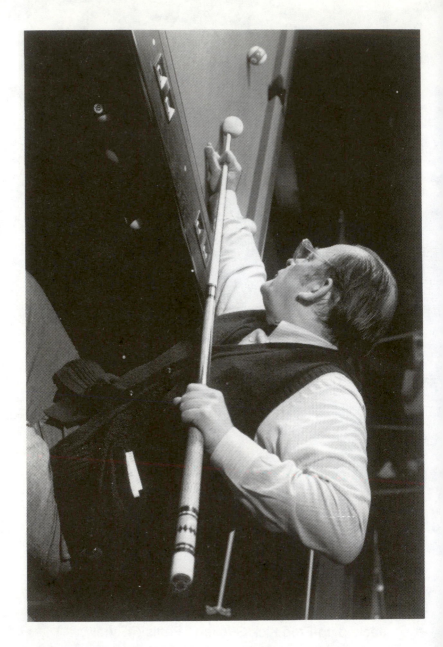

Modified Side Arm Stroke-C.Raftis

Side Arm Stroke-C.Raftis

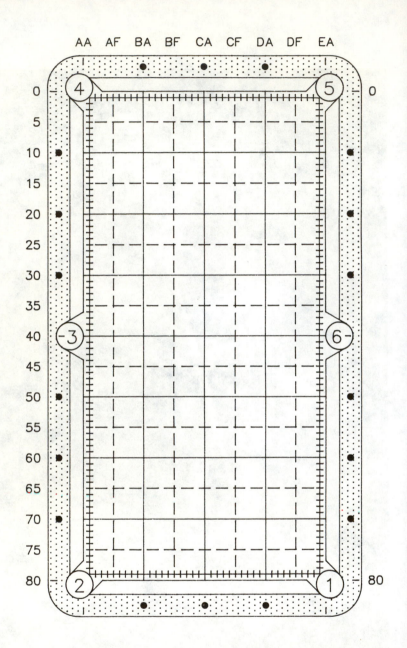

ALL PURPOSE CHART

MECHANICAL AIDS

All purpose billiard chart   312

Corner Blow Up of All Purpose Chart   314

Billiard Protractor   315

How to use the Protractor 1   316

How to use the Protractor 2   317

How to use the Protractor 3   318

Richard Clancy addressing c.b.   -back view

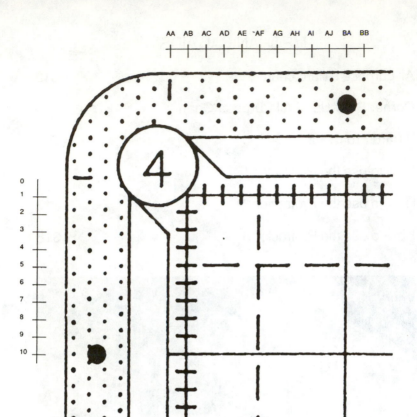

Illustrated Blow -up of the upper left hand corner of the All Purpose Chart. This blow-up of the corner identifies the lines on the all purpose chart so that the chart may be used to identify ball positions as they would appear on a pool table. By having a means to identify the ball positions then a player in one city or location could play a player in another city by means of radio, T.V. or telephone communication.

Another reason for identifying the ball positions is that if a listener at home listening to a radio broadcast of a pool game would have available an all purpose pool chart, then by writing the ball numbers in position on the chart, the listener could follow the progress of the pool game. The same listener could also follow instructions for making a variety of shot patterns for practicing at home.

The illustration show the long lines of the table as AA through AJ and then a continuation starting at BA through BB. The natural continuation would be BA through BJ; then CA through CJ; DA through DJ; and finally the last long line that is shown on the all purpose chart as EA.

The short across the table lines are shown on the illustration as one through ten. The continuation would then be eleven through eighty. By using these identifications any ball or balls located on a pool table could be transferred to a pool table chart for purposes of identification, instruction or computation. The pockets are also identified for the same reason.

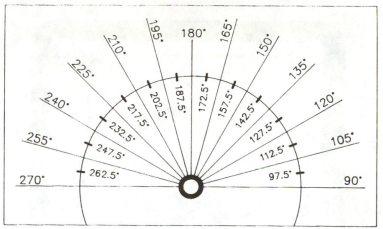

Billiard Protractor

The billiard protractor needs to be photocopied on transparency stock. Then locate the object ball on the all purpose chart. Next determine the best entry into the pocket. On an extended line from the pocket to the center of the object ball add a phantom cue ball. Now draw a line through the centers of the two cue balls, extend the line to the rail. Draw another line through the phantom cue ball, the object ball and the desired pocket entry. Now measure the angle. Research the angle on the ball charts. The ball chart also shows the amount of ball cover which may be useful in making the shot pattern.

Greg Dudzinski addressing cue ball-side view

313

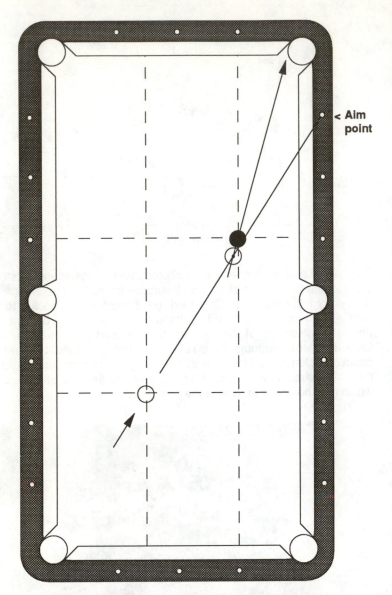

< Aim
point

Advanced and Expert: How to use protractor

Place balls in position as shown. Locate the desired entry into the pocket. Draw a line from the entry through the object ball. Extend the line one ball distant. Now locate the phantom cue ball. Draw a line through the two cue balls. Place the 180° line of protractor over this line. Reference the angle at 195°. The angle 195° is also known as a three fourths all hit or cut.

314

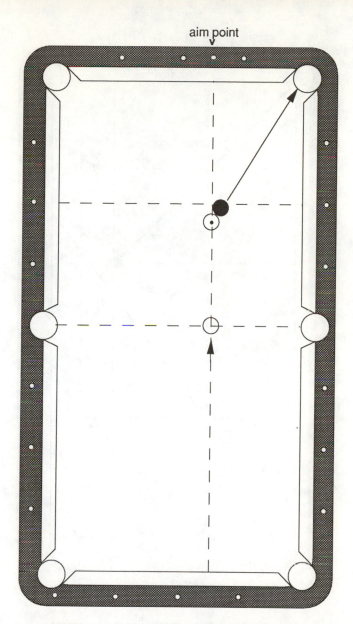

aim point

Advanced and Expert: Use of Protractor

Position balls as shown. Now follow the next four steps. Step one: Draw a line from the desired opening of the pocket through the center of the object ball. Step two: Where the line extends on the other side of the object ball, place a phantom cue ball. Step three: Draw a line throught the centers of the two cue balls. Step four: Measure the angle where the lines connect. Step five: Examine the ball charts to reference the degree of angle. Step six: Use the ball shadow to properly align the shot pattern. This example is 150° and a half ball cut. Verified.

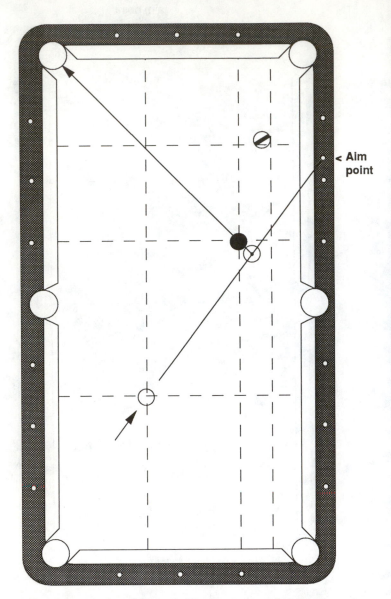

< Aim point

Advanced and Expert: How to use protractor

Place balls in position as shown. Locate the desired entry into the pocket opening. Draw a line from that desired entry through the object ball. Extend the line one ball distant. Now locate the phantom cue ball. Now draw a line through the two cue balls. Place the 180° line of protractor over this reference line. The angle then is 262 1/2°. The angle 262 1/2° angle is also known as a thin hit.

SPECIAL INDEX-THE ESSENCE OF THE BOOK

ANGLE of incidence equals the angle of reflection: explained p.37; examples pp.78-83; 123, 124, 204, 205, 217.

BANKS: explained pp.37,40,43; examples pp.121-131, 259, 267-269, 273, 280.

CHALKING: explained p.9; examples pp. 2, 48 and 76.

DIAMOND system: explained pp. 85,195; examples pp. 82-85, 88, 89, 195-203, 206, 267.

DRAW: explained p.40; examples pp. 23,51, 164-173, 211-215.

HALF ball hit: explained p.53; examples pp. 55, 57, 63, 66, 118, 317.

JACKED up: explained pp.42,304; examples pp.304-309.

JUMP shot: explained p.43; examples 245-248, 250-253.

KICKS: explained p.43; calculations pp. 156, 2311, 232, 134, 217, 150, 151; examples pp. 78-84, 86-89, 120, 132-158, 164-166, 168-170, 172, 181, 196-244, 249, 254-258, 264, 265, 276-279, 281, 282.

KISSES: examples pp. 160-163, 270-272.

MECHANICAL BRIDGE: explained p.9; examples pp. 30-35, 43 and 46.

POWER STROKE: explained p.3; examples pp. 88, 89 and 200.

REVERSE english: examples pp.126, 127, 131, 136, 137, 143, 154, 158, 169, 213, 216, 238, 260, 279, 280.

RIFLYING: explained pp. 12, 38, 45; examples pp. ii, iii, 10, 14, 15, 47, 74, 77, 176, 177, 192, 193, 266, 287, 313, 315.

RUNNING english: examples pp. 128, 129, 130, 135, 138, 139, 140, 152, 153, 157, 209, 218-223, 225-230, 233-237, 240, 241, 244, 259, 261, 263-265, 277, 278, 281, 282.

SIDE arm stroke: explained pp 3,5; example pp.i, 36, 311.

SLIP stroke: explained pp 12,46; example p.36.

SPINNERS: examples pp. 120, 121, 255-258.

STRAIGHT ins: explained p.53; examples pp 56, 90, 91.

SYSTEMS: Bank shot p.124, Cuts pp.93, 94, 118, 119, 288; Diamond pp.85, 89; Draws pp. 173, 213; Follow shot p.150; Kick shot pp. 43, 134, 150, 151, 156, 217, 231, 232; Jump shot pp. 247, 253; Kiss shot pp. 160-162; spinners pp. 255, 256; Straight ins pp. 90, 911.

THIN hit: explained p. 53; examples pp. 54, 59, 262, 263, 318.

DIAGRAM INDEX

1	Adv and Exp.-Fancy shots-Cross corner bank	267
2	Adv and Expert-Daimond System-2 rail kick	203
3	Adv and Expert-Kick Shot-2 rails long side	205
4	Adv and Expert-Diamond Sys.-3 rail ball tracks	195
5	Adv.and Exp.-Diamond Sys.-EXPLANATION	89
6	Beg & Inter.-ANGLE INCIDENCE = REFLEC.	81
7	Beg & Intermediates-Draw Kick-1 rail corner	166
8	Beg & Intermediates-Draw Kick-1 rail corner	165
9	Adv and Expert-Diamond Sys.-2 rails side	199
10	Adv and Expert-Kick-EXT. TABLE.THEORY	231
11	Adv and Expert-Kick Shot-2 rails into corner	228
12	Adv and Expert-Fancy -3 balls into 2 pockets	269
13	Adv and Expert-Dead Ball Hit-Kick Shot	145
14	Adv and Expert-Fancy Shots-3 balls 3 pockets	270
15	Adv and Expert-Kick Shot-2 rails corner	229
16	Adv and Expert-Kick Shot-2 rails corner	226
17	Adv and Expert-Fancy-3 balls in 1 pocket	272
18	Adv and Expert-USE OF PROTRACTOR	227
20	Adv and Expert-Cut Shots-Rail first spinner	261
21	Adv and Expert-Cut Shots-2 rail kick corner	230
22	Adv and Expert-O.B. INFLUENCED BY ENG.	259
23	Adv and Expert-Diamond System-3 rail kick	201
24	Adv and Expert-Diamond System-3 rail kick	200
25	Adv and Expert-Diamond System-2 rails side	206
26	Beg & Intermediates-Kick Shot-1 across side	79
27	Beg & Intermediates-Kick Shot-1 across corner	78
28	Beg.& Intermediates-Kick Shot-2 rails corner	83
29	Beg & Intermediates-Kick Shot-2 rails side	86
30	Beg & Intermediates-Kick Shot-2 rails corner	87
32	Beg. & Inter.-DIAMOND SYS.-EXPLANATION	85
33	Beginners & Intermediates-Kiss Shot-Draw	160
34	Beginners & Intermediates-Kiss Shot-Follow	162
35	Beg & Inter.-Cut -ANGLE OF DEVIATION	119
36	Beg & Intermediates-Cut-THE HALF BALL HIT	118
37	Beg.& Intermediates-Bank Shot-1 rail side	125
38	Beg & Intermediates-Kiss Shot-Dead Ball Hit	161

39	Beg & Intermediates-Cut Shot-Corner Pocket	117
40	Beg & Intermediates-Cut Shot-Corner Pocket	101
41	Beg & Intermediates-Cut Shot-Corner Pocket	111
42	Beg & Intermediates-Cut Shot-Corner Pocket	113
43	Beg & Intermediates-Cut Shot-Corner Pocket	99
44	Beg & Intermediates-Cut Shot-Corner Pocket	97
45	Beg & Intermediates-Cut Shot-Side Pocket	96
46	Beg & Intermediates-Cut Shot-Corner Pocket	95
47	Beg & Intermediates-Cut Shot-Side Pocket	92
48	Beg & Intermediates-Cut Shot-Corner Pocket	116
49	Beg & Intermediates-Cut Shot-Corner Pocket	115
50	Beg & Intermediates-Cut Shot-Corner Pocket	114
51	Beg & Intermediates-Cut Shot-Corner Pocket	107
52	Beg & Intermediates-Cut Shot-Corner Pocket	112
53	Beg & Intermediates-Cut Shot-Corner Pocket	103
54	Beg & Intermediates-Cut Shot-Corner Pocket	105
55	Beg & Intermediates-Cut Shot-Corner Pocket	109
56	Beg & Inter.-The Spinner-1 rail bank kick	120
58	Beg & Inter.-Kick Shot-SYSTEM EXPLAINED	156
59	Beg & Inter.-Nip Draw-Kick into corner	167
61	Beg & Inter.-Cuts-ANGLE DEV.=ANGLE ADJ.	93
62	Beg & Inter.-Cut Shots-SYS. INSTRUCTION	94
63	Beg & Intermediates-Kick Shot-1 rail corner	143
64	Beg & Intermediates-Kick Shot-1 rail corner	137
65	Beg & Intermediates-Kick Shot-1 rail into side	136
67	Adv.and Expert-Draw Curve-Kick into corner	216
68	Beg & Inter.-Combination Shot-Corner	159
70	Beg & Intermediates-Kick Shot-1 rail corner	139
71	Beg.& Intermediates-Kick Shot-1 rail corner	140
72	Adv and Expert-Kick -2 rails across corner	218
73	Adv and Expert-Kick Shot-One rail into corner	219
74	Adv.and Expert-Draw Shot-Kick into corner	208
75	Adv and Expert-Draw Shot-Kick into corner	210
76	Adv and Expert-Draw Shot-Kick into corner	209
77	Adv and Expert-Draw Shot-Kick into corner	215
78	Adv and Expert-Draw Shot-Kick into corner	213
79	Adv and Expert-Draw Shot-Kick into corner	207
80	Adv and Expert-The Spinner-1 rail into corner	255
81	Adv and Exp.-The Spinner-1 rail across corner	256
82	Beg & Intermediates-Bank Shot-1 rail corner	128

83	Beg & Intermediates-Bank Shot-1 rail side	123
84	Beg & Intermediates-Bank Shot-1 rail corner	127
85	Beg & Intermediates-Bank -SYS. EXPLAINED	124
86	Beg.& Inter.-Bank Shot-1 rail across side	126
87	Beg & Inter.-Bank Shot-1 rail long corner	130
88	Beg & Intermediates-Bank Shot-1 rail corner	131
89	Beg & Intermediates-Bank -3 rails long side	122
90	Beg & Inter.-Bank -INFLUENCE OF ENGLISH	121
91	Beg & Intermediates-Kick -SYS. INSTRUCTION	134
92	Beg & Intermediates-Kick Shot-1 rail corner	138
93	Beg & Intermediates-Kick -2 rails into corner	157
94	Beg & Intermediates-Kick -Two rails into side	158
95	Beg & Intermediates-Kick Shot-1 rail side	135
96	Beg.& Intermediates-Kick Shot-2 rails corner	155
97	Beg.& Intermediates-Kick Shot-2 rails corner	152
98	Beg.& Intermediates-Kick Shot-1 rail.corner	153
99	Beg & Inter.-Kick Shot-Soft draw into corner	146
100	Beg & Intermediates-Kick -Follow into corner	147
101	Beg.& Intermediates-Kick -Follow into corner	148
102	Beg & Intermediates-Kick -Follow into corner	149
103	Beg & Intermediates-Kick Shot-1 rail corner	142
104	Beg & Intermediates-Kick Shot-1 rail corner	41
105	Beg & Intermediates-Kick Shot-1 rail into side	132
106	Beg & Intermediates-Kick Shot-1 rail corner	133
107	Beg & Intermediates-Kick Shot-1 rail corner	144
108	Beg.& Inter.-Break Shot-SYS. INSTRUCTION	188
109	Beg & Inter.-Break Shot-SYS. INSTRUCTION	181
110	Beg & Inter.-Straight In-SYS. INSTRUCTION	91
111	Beg.& Inter.-Straight In-SYS. INSTRUCTION	90
112	Beg & Intermediates-Draw -Kick into corner	170
113	Beg & Intermediates-Draw -Cut into corner	171
114	Beg & Inter.-Draw -INFLUENCE OF ENGLISH	169
115	Beg & Intermediates-Draw -Kick into corner	172
116	Beg & Inter.-Draw Shot-SYS. INSTRUCTION	173
117	Beg & Intermediates-Kiss Shot-Kick into corner	163
119	Adv and Expert-Jump Draw- INSTRUCTION	251
120	Adv and Expert-Fancy Shots-Time shot corner	280
121	Beg & Intermediates-Kick Shot-1 rail into corner	154
122	Advanced and Expert-Bank -One rail corner	129
124	Adv and Expert-Kick Shot-One rail into corner	244

125	Adv and Expert-Kick Shot-Three rails into ball	241
126	Adv and Exp.-Kick Shot-Five rails into corner	243
127	Adv and Expert-Kick Shot-1 rail across corner	240
128	Adv. and Expert-Kick Shot-UMBRELLA SHOT	239
129	Advanced and Expert-Kick Shot-Rail First	238
130	Advanced and Expert-Kick Shot-Rail First	237
131	Advanced and Expert-Kick Shot-Rail First	236
132	Adv and Expert-Kick Shot-One rail into corner	235
133	Adv and Expert-Kick Shot-One rail into corner	234
134	Adv and Expert-Kick Shot-Four rails into corner	233
135	Adv and Expert-Kick Shot-Five rails into corner	225
136	Adv and Expert-Kick Shot-SYS. INSTRUCTION	232
137	Adv and Expert-Kick Shot-One rail into corner	224
138	Adv and Expert-Kick Shot-3 rails into corner	223
139	Adv and Exp.-Kick Shot-Two rails into corner	222
140	Adv and Expert-Kick Shot-3 rails into corner	221
141	Adv and Exp.-Kick Shot-Five rails into corner	220
142	Adv and Expert-Kick -SYSTEM INSTRUCTION	217
143	Adv and Expert-Draw Shot-Short follow through	211
144	Adv and Expert-Position Shot-High Ball Curve	258
145	Advanced and Expert-Position Shot-Soft Draw	257
146	Adv and Expert-Jump Shot- INSTRUCTION	247
147	Adv. and Expert-The Spinner- INSTRUCTION	253
148	Adv. and Expert-The Spinner-SYSTEM INSTR.	254
149	Adv and Expert-Daimond System-3 rails corner	197
150	Adv and Exp.-Fancy Shots-Kick, curve corner	277
151	Adv and Expert-Fancy Shots-3 balls 3 pockets	275
152	Adv and Expert-Fancy Shots-6 balls 6 pockets	273
153	Adv and Expert-Fancy Shots-Machine Gun	276
154	Beg & Inter.-Fancy Shots-Dropped Rack	265
155	Adv and Exp.-Fancy Shots-4 balls 4 pockets	278
156	Adv and Exp.-Fancy Shots-3 balls 3 pockets	279
157	Adv and Expert-Time Shot-Difficult but possible	263
158	Adv. and Expert-Time Shot-A good possibility	262
159	Beg & Intermediates-Kick -SYS. INSTRUCTION	151
160	Beg.& Intermediates-Kick -SYS. INSTRUCTION	150
161	Beg & Intermediates-Kick Shot-Three rails side	84

ILLUSTRATION AND PRINCIPLES

Cue Ball Striking Points	52
Cut Shots 1	54
Cut shots 2	55
Cut Shots 3	56
Cut Shots 4	57
Cut Shots 5	58
Cut Shots 6	59
Cut Shot Reference 1	60
Cut Shot Reference 2	61
Cut Shot Reference 3	62
Cut Shot Reference 4	63
Cut Shot Reference 5	64
Cut Shot Reference 6	65
Cut Shot Reference 7	66
Cut Shot Reference 8	67
Cut Shot Reference 9	68
Cut Shot Reference 10	69
Cut Shots-Angle Dev. = Ang. Incidence	286
Angle Study	293
Force Study	294
Big Ball Principle	295
Push Shot Principle	296
Speed Practice	297
Hit Practice	298
Speed Chart	70

PHOTO INDEX 'A'

Page	Photo	View
i	W.C. player using side arm stroke-	Side
iv	Portrait of a lady player-Kristie Ann	Front
vi	Portrait of a lady player-Carol	Front
2	Lady chalking cue-Carol	Front
4	Child holding a cue-Chrissy	Front
6	Pocket Billiard Equipment	Top
14	Ladie's line up-Kristie Ann	Side
15	Ladie's Stance-Kristie Ann	Side
16	Lady in Stroking Position-Carol	Front
17	Lady in Stroking Position-Carol	Side
18	Ladie's Stance-Carol	Back
19	Child Stroking Ball-Clint	Side
20	Pendulum Stroking Position-C.Raftis	Rear
21	Bridge Hand-Club Fist for Follow	Front
22	Bridge Hand-Club Fist for Center	Front
23	Bridge Hand-Club Fist for Draw	Front
24	Bridge Hand-Over athe Thumb	Side
25	Bridge Hand-Made famous by "Hoppe"	Side
26	Bridge Hand-Overlapping Finger	Side
27	Bridge Hand-Over the Thumb	Side
28	Bridge Hand-Showing the "V" Groove	Side
29	Bridge Hand-For Over a Ball	Front
30	Mechanical Bridge-Over a Ball	Close Up
31	Mechanical Bridge-Long Reach	Front
32	Child utilizing Milk Crate-Chrissy	Front
33	Mechanical Bridge-Over a Ball	Front
34	Mechanical Bridge-Lady-Carol	Close Up
35	Mechanical Bridge-Lady-Carol	Side
36	The "Slip" Stroke-C.Raftis	Rear
48	Chalking the Tip-C.Raftis	Front
72	Child Holding a Cue-Clint	Front
74	Position of the Head-Kristie Ann	Front
76	Lady Holding a cue-Carol	Close Up
80	Beg. and Intermediate-1 rail kick#6	O.H.
82	Beg. and Intermediate-Kick Shot#28	O.H.
88	Beg. and Intermediate-3 rail kick #5	O.H.

98	Beg. and Intermediate-Cut Shots #43	O.H.
100	Beg. and Intermediate-Cut Shots #40	O.H.
102	Beg. and Intermediate-Cut Shots #53	O.H.
104	Beg. and Intermediate-Cut Shots #54	O.H.
106	Beg. and Intermediate-Cut Shots #51	O.H.
108	Beg. and Intermediate-Cut Shots #55	O.H.
110	Beg. and Intermediate-Cut Shots #41	O.H.
164	Beg. and Intermediate-Cross Corner #8	O.H.
168	Beg. and Intermediate-Draw Shot #114	O.H.
196	Adv. and Expert-Diamond System #149	O.H.
198	Adv. and Expert-2 rail kick #9	O.H.
202	Adv. and Expert-2 rail Kick #2	O.H.
204	Adv. and Expert-1 rail kick #3	O.H.
212	Adv. and Expert-Draw Shot #78	O.H.
214	Adv. and Expert-Draw Shot #77	O.H.
242	Adv. and Expert-5 rail kick #126	O.H.
248	Adv. and Expert-The Jump Shot #146	O.H.
250	Adv. and Expert-The Jump Draw #119	O.H.
252	Adv. and Expert-The Spinner #147	O.H.
260	Adv. and Expert-Cut Shots #20	O.H.
266	Adv. and Expert-Fancy Shots #1	O.H.
268	Adv. and Expert-Fancy Shots #12	O.H.
272	Adv. and Expert-Fancy Shots #152	O.H.
274	Adv. and Expert-Fancy Shots #151	O.H.
291	Ball Position at Cushion-Soft Hit	Front
292	Ball Position at Cushion-Hard Hit	Front
303	Jacked-up; Cue under chin	Front
304	Jacked-up; Cue over head	Top
305	Jacked-up; Cue over head	Front
306	Jacked-up; Frog Kick Stroke	Top
307	Jacked-up; Frog Kick Stroke	Front
308	Modified Side Arm Stroke	Rear
309	Side Arm Stroke-C.Raftis	Rear

PHOTO INDEX 'B'

1 Greg Dudzinski addressing c b.-back view — 177
2 Greg Dudzinski addressing c b.-back view — 177
3 Greg Dudzinski addressing c b.-side view — 315
4 Greg Dudzinski follow through-angle view — i i
5 Dominic Zito addressing c b.-side view — 178
6 Dominic Zito addressing c b.-angle view — i i i
7 Dominic Zito follow through-front view — 186
8 Dominic Zito addressing c b.-front view — 285
9 Dominic Zito addressing c b.-angle view — 178
10 Dominic Zito using rail bridge-angle view — 195
11 Benjamin Jardin's back swing-side view — 193
12 Benjamin Jardin addressing c b.-s view — 264
13 Benjamin Jardin's follow through-s view — 194
14 Benjamin Jardin prior to stroke-s view — 000
15 Benjamin Jardin's break shot-front view — 181
16 Benjamin Jardin prior to stroke-frt view — 194
17 Richard Clancy prior to stroke-side view — 77
18 Richard Clancy addressing c b.-back view — 311
19 Richard Clancy's follow through-angle v. — 000
20 John Beyerlin's follow through-side view — 10
21 John Beyerlin's follow through-angle v — 176
22 John Beyerlin's follow through-side view — 47
23 Jeff Hoeksema addressing c b.-frt view — 245
24 Jeff Hoeksema prior to stroke-frt view — 246
25 Jeff Hoeksema addressing c b.-side view — 247
26 Jeff Hoeksema prior to stroke-side view — 247